PRAISE FOR
LET'S RI[...]

"Sonny Barger spreads the gospel of two wheels in *Let's Ride.* He is the rare rider who could write such a book with authority."   —*Los Angeles Times*

"The charm of *Let's Ride: Sonny Barger's Guide to Motorcycling* comes from the common sense conclusions peppered with the author's real life events. Sonny Barger's stories and experiences bring a dimension lost in many motorcycle books: the feel of seasoned advice from a riding buddy sitting on the next bar stool. One of the joys of riding is the wealth of knowledge so freely and enjoyably shared at motorcycle events and bike nights among fellow bikers. *Let's Ride* captures this perfectly."
     —*Clutch and Chrome*

"*Let's Ride* is the new authoritative guide to motorcycling and rider safety from Sonny Barger, the famous 'leader of the pack.'"   —BikerNews.org

"*Let's Ride* provides a broad spectrum of information. Informative, instructive, and entertaining—there is something for everyone."
     —CycleMatters.com

"Offers up a lifetime of bike-riding wisdom you just can't argue with."   —*Biker Chick News*

ABOUT THE AUTHORS

RALPH "SONNY" BARGER is the author of *Hell's Angel: The Life and Times of Sonny Barger and the Hell's Angels Motorcycle Club*. A master mechanic who has owned and operated his own bike shops, he currently lives in Arizona, where he rides every day.

DARWIN HOLMSTROM, senior editor at Motorbooks International, has written or cowritten more than a dozen books on motorcycles, including *The Harley-Davidson Motor Co. Archive Collection*, *BMW Motorcycles*, and *The Complete Idiot's Guide to Motorcycles*.

LET'S RIDE

ALSO BY SONNY BARGER

Hell's Angel: The Life and Times of Sonny Barger
and the Hell's Angels Motorcycle Club

Ridin' High, Livin' Free: Hell-Raising Motorcycle
Stories

Dead in 5 Heartbeats: A Novel

Freedom: Credos from the Road

6 Chambers, 1 Bullet: A Novel

LET'S RIDE

Sonny Barger's Guide to Motorcycling

Sonny Barger with
Darwin Holmstrom

HARPER

NEW YORK · LONDON · TORONTO · SYDNEY

HARPER

Grateful acknowledgment is made to the following for the photographs that appear in this book. Page xiv: © by Dieter Rebmann; pages 18 and 54: © by Sonny Barger Productions; page 92: © by Gene Anthony; page 122: © by Tina Hager; page 176: © by Nicolas Syracuse; page 198: photograph by Jinushi © by Free&Easy magazine; page 230: photograph by Clay Garder © by Sonny Barger Productions; page 261: photograph by Paul Hatton © by Thunder Roads Arizona.

A hardcover edition of this book was published in 2010 by William Morrow, an imprint of HarperCollins Publishers.

FIRST HARPER PAPERBACK PUBLISHED 2011.

Designed by Jamie Lynn Kerner

Library of Congress Cataloging-in-Publication Data has been applied for.

ISBN 978-0-06-196427-5

HB 03.25.2023

I would like to dedicate this to my wife, Zorana, who also rides. She has been riding for seven years and now rides a 2008 Street Glide. No, I did not even attempt to teach her to ride.

—Sonny Barger

I would like to thank Fritz Clapp for hooking me up with this project, Jim Fitzgerald for being the driving force that made it happen, and Zorana, who helped coordinate the creation of the book. I'd like to thank Ken Fund and Zack Miller at Motorbooks for letting me do this project, and also our editor Peter Hubbard and the rest of the crew at William Morrow/HarperCollins. I'd especially like to thank Sonny, whose enthusiasm for motorcycles provided the energy for this book. Sonny is, without question, the most dedicated motorcyclist I have ever met. I also want to thank my family, in particular my wife, Pat, and my father, Dean, who are also my best friends. I'd like to dedicate this book to my mother, JoAnne, who passed away while we were writing the book.

—Darwin Holmstrom

CONTENTS

INTRODUCTION: WHY RIDE?   1

**I. DISSECTING THE BEAST:
THE ANATOMY OF A MOTORCYCLE**   19

Putting the Motor in the Cycle   20

    The Crankcase   22

    The Cylinder Block(s)   23

    The Pistons . . . and Fuel Intake System   25

The Four Strokes of a Four-Stroke   26

Redlining   27

Engine Types   30

    Single Cylinders   32

    V-Twins   33

    Twisting Force   35

    L-Twins   36

    Parallel Twins   37

    Opposed Twins, Fours, and Sixes   38

    Inline Triples   40

    Inline Fours   42

    V-Fours   45

Final Drive Assembly   46

Electrical Systems   48

Transmissions   49

Saddles   50

Wind Protection   50

Riding Position   51

2. TYPES OF BIKES: WHAT TO RIDE   55

On-Road Versus Off-Road   58

Antique Motorcycles   60

Choppers and Bobbers   61

Managing Your Machine   66

How Small Is Too Small?   69

Rising Fatalities   70

Specific Types of Motorcycles   71

    Dual Sports   72

    Supermotards   75

    Cruisers   76

    Touring Bikes   79

    Sport-Tourers   81

    Sport Bikes   84

    Standards   88

3. THE FUNDAMENTALS OF RIDING   93

The Six Basic Controls   96

Secondary Controls   97

Preride Inspection   99

Checking Tires   101

Countersteering   103

Cranking It Over   105

Engaging the Clutch   109

Hitting the Brakes   110

Taking Off   112

Gearing Up   114
    Helmets   115
    Riding Jackets and Pants   118
    Boots and Gloves   119

4. EVALUATING A USED MOTORCYCLE   123

Why Buy a Used Motorcycle?   123

A Cautionary Note About Resurrecting Wrecks   126

Mechanical Inspection   128

Dealerships Versus the Private Seller   130

Getting Down to Business   132

The Cosmetic Evaluation   134
    Does It Shine?   134
    What Do Dents Mean?   136

A Part-by-Part Guide to Inspecting a Used Motorcycle   139
    The Electrics   140
    The Chassis   146

Steering Head Bearings 149
Tires 150
Frames 152
Swingarms/Rear Suspensions 153
The Final Drive 156
Brakes 159
Checking the Oil 165

The Road Test 168

5. BUYING A BIKE 177

Pricing a Used Motorcycle 178

Financing a Bike 179

Motorcycle Insurance 181

Buying a New Motorcycle 185

Beware of "Beta Testing" New Bikes 186

Finding a Good Motorcycle Shop 188

The Service Department 190

Final Negotiations 193

Pulling the Trigger 195

6. ADVANCED RIDING TECHNIQUES 199

Situational Awareness 200

Defeating Road Hazards 205

Making Yourself Visible 212

Zones of Awareness 214

Intersections   216

Blind Spots   219

The Soft Lane Change   220

Preserving Safe Space   222

Braking Practice   225

Riding in the Rain   227

7. **LIVING WITH A MOTORCYCLE**   231

Basic Maintenance   232

Changing Oil   239

Maintaining Your Chain   242

Touring   246

Packing for a Trip   249

Planning a Trip   250

Clubs   253

Mom-and-Pop Clubs   256

Clubs for the Other Ninety-eight Percent   258

APPENDIX: MOTORCYCLE RESOURCES   263

X. RIDING WITH A MOTORCYCLE

APPENDIX: MOTORCYCLE RESOURCES

LET'S RIDE

INTRODUCTION
Why Ride?

Back in the 1970s people used to say: "Ride hard, die young, and leave a good-looking corpse." People said a lot of stupid things in those days. I'm in my seventies today, and that saying seems idiotic to me now. I've got a better plan: ride smart, live long, and die of old age. I take good care of myself. I eat a healthy diet, I exercise every day, and I ride safe. I do this not because I'm afraid of dying. I do it because the longer I stay healthy, the longer I can ride motor-cycles.

If there's one thing I want you to know about me, it's that I love to ride. A lot of people know a lot about me, mostly because I've written one book about my life and another about my philosophy. Other people *think* they know me because so much has been written about me over the past half century. Some of it is true, but most is bullshit. And none of it is relevant here; the only thing that matters is that I love motorcycles. You do, too, or you wouldn't be reading this book.

Most motorcycle owners really aren't serious riders. They ride maybe once or twice on a weekend and only when the sun is out. They don't get up in the morning and ride to work in the cold or rain. More often than not they get in their cars instead of on their bikes.

That's not me. When it comes to a bike or a car, there is no choice. Unless I'm getting something that's too big to haul on my bike, like feed for my horses, I take the bike every time. Many times in my life I haven't even owned a car, but I always had a bike. There have been many times when I couldn't afford both a car and a motorcycle, so I always chose a bike over a car. My family and I have even had to shop for groceries on a motorcycle, but that's the way I prefer it.

Becoming a serious rider is no easy thing to do. It takes dedication and hard work, but there's not a lot you can do about it if riding motorcycles is in your blood as it is in mine. You just have to suck it up and do the work.

I've been fascinated with motorcycles as early as I can remember. As a child, I loved watching bikes roar by our house. We lived on Seventeenth Street in East Oakland, which was still a small town back in the 1940s, and our house was near a stop sign that everyone used to run. Motorcycle cops used to sit in a vacant lot by my home and wait for unsuspecting people to run the stop sign. I'd stand for hours watching the cops take off after traffic violators. The sound of their motors made me feel good.

When I was finally old enough to ride, I got a little Cushman scooter. I never got sick of riding it around our neighborhood. I loved the sound, the feel of the wind against my body. After I saw *The Wild One,* I knew I wanted a real motorcycle. When I was discharged from the army in 1956, the Bohemian thing was big in the Bay Area. I had to decide whether I was going to be a beatnik or a motorcyclist. I picked motorcycles. I'm glad I did because motorcycles are still around while the beatniks are long gone.

I bought a 1937 Indian Scout as soon as I returned home from the army. At that time, I was too young to legally own a motorcycle in the state of California, so I had to buy it in my older sister's name. Despite my age, back in the 1950s no one cared if I rode it; if it ran, you could ride it, whether you had a license or not.

The Scout ran, but it wasn't in excellent shape. It was a 45-cubic-inch (750-cc) side-valve V-twin that put out about 25 horsepower on a good day. If you really cranked on it, it might have hit 75 miles per hour when it was in its prime, but by the time I bought it, its best days were long past and it wasn't reliable enough to take out on the highway. During the short time I owned it, I never left the city of Oakland.

Within a few months I had my first Harley, a 1936 Knucklehead that cost me $125, tax included. This was a much better machine, a 61-cubic-inch bike that was well suited for longer trips. I rebuilt it and put in cylinder barrels and a flywheel from a 74-cubic-inch Knucklehead. Later I stroked it by putting in a flywheel from an 80-cubic-inch Flathead. I rode that bike all over California. When the stroked Knuckle engine blew up, I built a 1958 Panhead motor up to 80 inches and rode that until I traded it in for a brand-new 1961 XLCH Sportster. I got $500 for my Knuckle-Pan and still owed $400 on the new Sportster, which seemed like an impossible amount of money back then. But it was worth it. Sportsters were the hottest bikes you could buy at the time. They ran circles around the Big Twins. I rode XLs for seven years.

I've never been without a bike since that Indian Scout. That was more than fifty years ago, and I enjoy riding motorcycles today as much as I did when I was a kid. It's still the only way I travel.

If you're anything like I was and you want to ride a motorcycle no matter what, it's time to quit thinking and start doing. Jump in, and swim. I'll explain in the following chapters what you need to do to make that happen, but throughout the book I'm going to stress the importance of getting proper training. Don't let friends or family members teach you to ride: do it right and take a riding class. We'll talk about the types of classes that are available in the upcoming chapters, but for now all you need to know is that completing a motorcycle riding class will be the safest way to practice the skills we cover in *Let's Ride*.

● ● ●

RIDING A MOTORCYCLE IS EASIER SAID than done. Much of the rest of this book will tell you what to do once you decide to become a motorcycle rider, but the challenges will start before you ever fire up your engine for the first time. You're going to have to deal with the concerns of your loved ones. As soon as you tell people you're interested in riding motorcycles, you'll start to hear an endless stream of warnings, mostly some variation of "Motorcycles are dangerous!" This is true—motorcycles are dangerous, but hey, life itself is dangerous. Everything you ever do will be a risk to some degree. Even doing nothing is dangerous because you'll get soft and fat and then die of heart disease. Death, after all, is the only sure bet in life.

No matter what you do, someone somewhere will tell you it's dangerous. If you listened to every one of them, you would never do anything. You may crash your motorcycle and get hurt or killed, but you may fall off a curb and get run over by a bus, too, or tonight you could choke on a piece of fried chicken. Statistically, your bathtub might be just as dangerous as your motorcycle; thousands of people die from falling in their tubs every year, but no one tells you not to take a bath.

My sister and my dad both tried to talk me out of riding. My dad rode motorcycles with his friends, but when a good friend of his got hurt, Dad quit riding. He even stopped driving cars after that—he took a bus everywhere. He never stopped worrying about me, but he supported my decision to ride.

Only you can decide if the freedom and excitement a motorcycle can provide is worth the level of risk. If you're like me and motorcycling is in your blood, there's only one answer: "Yes."

I've done a lot of things that are more dangerous than riding a motorcycle. Smoking cigarettes came closer to killing me than riding any motorcycle has ever done. Abusing drugs gave me a heart attack when I was in my early forties. But riding motorcycles has kept me active and feeling young and alive over the years, so for me riding a motorcycle is more than worth the risks involved.

Once you've weighed the pros and cons of riding a motorcycle and decided the rewards are worth the risks, you need to do everything in your power to minimize those risks. Motorcycle riding *is* dangerous, but you can do a lot of things to make it safer. Much of the rest of this book discusses ways to avoid unnecessary risks and manage the risks you can't avoid. But first, let's discuss the rewards of motorcycling and dispel some of the myths that have grown up around bikers.

WHEN PEOPLE HEAR THAT YOU WANT to ride a motorcycle, they'll use every argument they can think of to try to talk you out of it, but they won't be able to argue with the fact that motorcycles are economical to own and operate. For starters, motorcycles are cheaper to buy than cars; the most expensive motorcycles cost about as much as the average family sedan, and the least expensive new motorcycles are cheaper than a used subcompact car. If you shop around, you can pick up a brand-new high-end motorcycle like a Victory Vegas for around $15,000, which is less than you'd pay for a new compact like a Honda Civic. You can get a decent, reliable motorcycle for under $5,000, and in some cases well under that amount. The only cars you can get for that price these days are about ready for the junkyard.

Motorcycles are fuel efficient as well. The largest, most luxurious motorcycle uses less gas than the lightest car. The most economical gas-powered cars average maybe 30 miles per gallon, and hybrid-powered cars don't get much more than 35 miles per gallon. Meanwhile the largest, most luxurious touring bikes usually get about 35–40 miles per gallon, and smaller bikes can easily get 50–60 miles per gallon. Gas prices traditionally fluctuate up and down, but with all the talk about "peak oil," I'll bet that, over the long run, fuel prices are going to trend a lot higher than they are today. The more they go up, the more money you'll save riding a motorcycle.

A lot of states also allow motorcycles to use their high-occupancy vehicle lanes, meaning you can get around on congested urban freeways more efficiently on a motorcycle than in a car. Another way to save money on a bike is in parking costs. Parking lots often charge less for motorcycles than they do for cars, which makes sense since motorcycles take up less space. If you're resourceful enough, you can even find places that let motorcycles park for free. For example, if you find a restaurant or other place of business owned by a motorcycle rider, he or she might let you park your bike in the alley or loading area behind the building. This brings up another benefit of motorcycling: a brotherhood exists among motorcycle riders.

● ● ●

As soon as you start riding a motorcycle, you'll find you are part of a larger community of motorcycle riders. The first thing you'll notice is that other motorcycle riders wave at you, even if you don't know them from Adam. Here's a word of advice—wave back. It doesn't matter if the other rider is some kid on a sport bike, some adventure-tourer traveling the globe on a big dual-purpose bike (we'll discuss the types of bikes and riders you'll meet later), or a member of a one-percenter club; that rider waving at you is acknowledging that the two of you are in this together. The least you could do is let the other rider know you get the message.

Waving goes back to the early days of riding. When I started riding, bikes were so unreliable that traveling the sixty miles from Oakland to San Jose was considered a big trip. You might only see one other motorcycle the whole way, so when you did, you waved at him. He might even stop and have a cup of coffee with you.

At least in part this brotherhood came about as the result of the antimotorcycle hysteria that infected the United States in the years after World War II. With communism spreading around the world and the Soviet Union getting an atomic bomb, you can't blame people for being scared of just about anything out of the ordinary, and back in those days riding a motorcycle was definitely unusual.

I first encountered this prejudice against motorcycles in 1958 while hanging out at a Doggie Diner on Twenty-third Avenue. I'd just been fired from my job and was sitting out in front of the diner when a straitlaced cop pulled up and told me that he'd been down to visit my boss the day before. I realized that he'd been the person who'd gotten me fired. From that day forward, it's gotten progressively worse. Just a couple of days ago I got a speeding ticket; the Immigration and Customs Enforcement (ICE) agent who pulled me over treated me like I was a damned dog. I've paid a lot of money in state and federal taxes, yet I get treated like that when I'm riding my motorcycle down a public highway.

BACK WHEN I STARTED RIDING, WHEN people spoke about a motorcycle, they were usually talking about either a Harley or an Indian. In some parts of California they might have been talking about a Triumph or some other Brit bike, but for most people in the United States the word *motorcycle* meant either a Harley or an Indian. With those bikes, you had to know how to fix them to ride them. Not just anyone with a fat wallet could walk into a motorcycle dealership and ride off on a new bike because in those days you spent as much time working on your bike as you did riding it. Every time you rode a bike, there was a fair chance something would go wrong before you got back home.

These days bikes are a lot more reliable and everyone has a cell phone; if something does go wrong, you can just call for help. But back then if your bike broke down, you had two choices: fix it or walk. To be a motorcycle rider in the early days of motorcycling meant that you had to be a decent motorcycle mechanic, too.

In 1958 I rode with a guy named Ernie Brown, who was the vice president of the club I was in at the time. We'd ridden down to Los Angeles and my transmission blew up. We were sitting on the side of the road when another motorcyclist named Vic Bettencourt stopped to help. It turned out that he was the president of a chapter of the same club.

I didn't even know our club had a chapter down there. We'd founded our club because we'd found a cool patch from a defunct club and we liked the patch. We didn't even know there were other chapters of the club. It was the first time we realized we were part of something bigger than just the club my friends and I had started. Vic took us to their clubhouse and put a new transmission in my bike. He also taught me a lot about what brotherhood was all about.

The tendency for bikes to break down all the time kept motorcycles off-limits for people who were trained to be things like schoolteachers and bank tellers instead of grease monkeys. It made riding a motorcycle more or less a blue-collar activity, which set up a class divide between riders and nonriders that wouldn't be torn down for generations.

ANOTHER REASON THAT MAINSTREAM AMERICAN citizens began to fear motorcycles was because of the press. As long as there have been newspapers, there've been newspaper publishers who've realized that fear sells newspapers. In the strange days following the Second World War, journalists had more fear to exploit than ever before. It didn't take much to scare the piss out of the average American in the late 1940s; anything that represented the unknown was frightening, and people who rode motorcycles represented an unknown quantity. The sight of a bunch of greasy-nailed motorcyclists roaring into a gas station was enough to make Mr. Average American wet his pants.

Being quick to pick up on anything that exploited the average American's fear of the unknown, the magazines and newspapers of the day (remember, this was back when hardly anyone had television) published stories on anything and everything that frightened people, whether it was Communist infiltrators, unidentified flying objects, or a bunch of guys out having a good time on their motorcycles. If something wasn't scary enough to sell newspapers and magazines, the newspapers and magazines would just stretch the truth until it was more sensational.

For the most part, I always get along with just about everyone I meet. People fear the unknown, but once they get to know you, they treat you the way you treat them. If you treat people with respect, they'll usually treat you with respect in return. If someone attacks me, I'm going to defend myself, but I don't go around doing things to scare people. But the problem comes when people read a lot of the crazy things that are written about me and think they should be afraid. And if it will sell papers and magazines, the press will print whatever crazy story they think people might believe.

That's exactly what they did with a motorcycle rally that got a little boisterous in the small town of

Hollister, California, over the Fourth of July holiday in 1947. About four thousand motorcycle riders came to town that weekend, mostly to attend races sponsored by the AMA (American Motorcyclist Association). That was a lot more people than the town expected and things got a little hectic.

Eyewitness reports tell of such things as motorcyclists throwing water balloons off balconies, popping wheelies on Main Street, and generally riding around whooping and hollering. There were a few drunken fights, and more than a little street racing, but other than a couple tools being stolen from a tire repair shop, there was no real crime to speak of. One guy was arrested for pissing in the radiator of a car that was overheating; when his buddy Wino Willy of the Booze Fighters Motorcycle Club went to bail him out of jail, he, too, was arrested for being drunk.

A total of twenty-nine people were arrested for drunkenness, indecent exposure, and traffic violations, but overall the motorcyclists were just a little rowdier than the cowboys were when the rodeo came to town. Finally one guy rode his motorcycle right into a bar, prompting the owner to call the California Highway Patrol, who cleared everyone out and put a stop to the party.

The Hollister event would have gone down in history as just another good Fourth of July party in a small town had not a photographer put a pile of empty beer bottles around a motorcycle and had a guy pose on the bike. He sold the resulting photo to *Life* magazine, which ran it with a short story about how hordes of motorcyclists were descending on the country hell-bent on destroying everything in their paths. Within weeks motorcycle riders replaced Communists as public enemy number one, which is more than a little ironic considering that most motorcyclists at the time were honorable patriots who had risked their lives serving their country in World War II. They just wanted to have a little fun, and they sure as hell had earned that right.

The *Life* magazine story inspired a guy named Frank Rooney to write a short story for *Harper's Magazine* called "The Cyclists' Raid." This piece of fiction became the basis for the 1953 film *The Wild One*. Mostly the film shows a bunch of people having a good time on motorcycles, but back then Johnny, played by Marlon Brando, seemed like the Antichrist to the average American, and the film helped to spread mistrust between motorcycle riders and non-motorcycle riders.

The film might have scared "average Americans" witless, but when my friends and I saw *The Wild One* as teenagers, we wanted to be just like Chino, the character played by Lee Marvin. Johnny seemed like he spent a lot of time feeling sorry for himself. I don't care what anyone says; Marlon Brando's character was a bully, and I don't like bullies. Whenever something happened, Marlon Brando said, "Me and my boys will take care of it." It was never: "I'll take care of it."

Chino had balls, and he knew how to have fun. Lee Marvin's character was like a real person. He wasn't out looking to push anyone around; he just wanted to ride his motorcycle and have a good time. He wanted everyone to be together as a group.

But as I say, most Americans didn't see the film

the way we did. Where we saw motorcyclists having a good time, they saw criminals who needed to be locked up. By the time I started riding motorcycles, motorcycle riding itself was practically a crime; not only did we have to be on constant vigil against careless car drivers, wild animals and dogs, and other hazards of the road, but we also had to watch out for the cops who would harass us at every opportunity just because of the mode of transportation we preferred. With this kind of pressure on us at all times, it made sense that we would seek the brotherhood found in motorcycle clubs.

BACK AROUND THE TURN OF THE twentieth century, people formed clubs around just about anything. There were clubs devoted to collecting butterflies, clubs devoted to examining dinosaur fossils, and clubs devoted to studying electricity. It only made sense that people would start forming motorcycle clubs almost as soon as Gottlieb Daimler first bolted a gasoline engine to his two-wheeled wooden Einspur to create the original motorcycle in 1885.

Motorcycle clubs remained popular throughout the first half of the twentieth century, but after World War II they became even more popular. Most able-bodied American men had served in the military during the war, and many of them missed the brotherhood they had shared with their fellow soldiers. Motorcycle clubs offered these veterans a way to re-create that camaraderie. By 1947, when the Hollister bash took place, there were dozens of clubs on the West Coast alone.

Just about everyone I know belongs to some sort of biking club. Riding alone is fun, but being part of a group provides advantages. With a group, you'll have someone to watch your back if something happens or help you if you go down. Plus it's nice to have someone to share the ride with. There are all sorts of clubs, and I encourage every rider to consider joining one for the brotherhood and camaraderie.

In 1957 six other guys and I started a chapter of the club I'm still in. Within six months I became president of our chapter, and I remained president for about thirty years. I'm still a member, but I haven't held an office in the club for more than twenty years. The type of club I'm in—a one-percenter club—probably isn't for everyone. No club is for everybody, but no matter what kind of riding you're interested in, you can find a motorcycle club that focuses on it.

I'VE SAVED MY PERSONAL FAVORITE PART of motorcycling for last: freedom. This subject is so important to me that I've written an entire book about it. I appreciate all the other benefits a motorcycle provides, especially the brotherhood of riders that forms around motorcycles, but for me in the end it all boils down to the freedom I find on a bike.

When I pop the gearshift lever on my bike into first and ride out onto the open road, I leave everything else behind. Before I get on my bike I might be worried about some deadline I have to meet, or some person I have to call, or some other obligation I have to fulfill, but once I ride out of my driveway, I leave all that other stuff behind. There's no room for it out on the road. I've got enough to worry about just trying to avoid all the other drivers yapping on their cell phones—there's no room for the petty worries that would be on my mind if I wasn't out on my bike.

At least I try to shed all those unimportant thoughts when I ride. Sometimes they creep in, but I do my best to avoid them because they distract me from the business at hand, which is not getting hurt or killed on my bike. Normally I do a pretty good job at clearing the unimportant crap from my mind and focusing on riding my bike. Because riding is such an intense activity, it demands your full attention. On a bike you're bombarded with all kinds of stuff coming at you, and I don't just mean other traffic. Riding reveals so many raw sights, sounds, and smells that they can overwhelm you. It can be a little intimidating at first, but I promise that riding will ultimately produce an amplified sense of being alive.

Once you let the experience of riding consume you and drive all the useless thoughts from your head, that's when you really start to enjoy the freedom of riding a bike. It doesn't matter if you're riding five miles or five hundred miles; time has little meaning when your head is in the act of riding and it's just you, your bike, and the road—at least until your ass starts to get sore and the pain interrupts your motorcycle meditation. Later in this book we'll talk about ways to prevent even that from being a problem.

RIDING REALLY IS A FORM OF meditation. Most religions have ways to help focus your thoughts—meditation, prayer, ceremonies—and in this way riding a motorcycle is a lot like a religion. I'm not going to talk about organized religions here because what people believe or don't believe is their own business. I don't talk to people about what I do or don't believe, and I appreciate when they don't talk to me about their beliefs. But when it comes to motorcycles, I figure that if you're reading this book you most likely have an interest in what I believe, at least as far as motorcycles are concerned.

And I believe that riding motorcycles is as good a religion as any, and probably better than most. For me, riding a motorcycle is like being part of a ceremony; it's a sort of transcendent experience some would call holy. I think a lot of my club brothers feel the same way. That's why we call going to our club meetings "going to church."

The rest of this book will cover the things you need to do to learn to ride a motorcycle, tell you how to buy the right motorcycle, teach you how to be comfortable and safe once you get it, and give you advice on what to do once you start riding. I hope that by getting the proper training, choosing a good motorcycle that suits your needs, and practicing good safety habits once you start riding, you'll stay strong and healthy and ride for many trouble-free years. Do that and you'll experience the pleasure that motorcycling has given me for more than half a century. Whether or not you join a club, if you love to ride a motorcycle, you are part of my church.

CHAPTER ONE

DISSECTING THE BEAST

The Anatomy of a Motorcycle

Motorcycles seem like they should be simple because there's really not much to them. You've got an engine, two wheels, tires, something to sit on, some controls to manage the machine, a tank for gasoline, and a frame to hold the whole works together.

In the early days of riding, the preceding description pretty much accounted for an entire motorcycle. The controls consisted of a cable going to a rudimentary carburetor, which was about as complex as a Turkish water pipe, and hopefully, a crude brake. The transmission was made up of a pulley that tightened a flat, smooth leather belt that ran from an output sprocket on the crankshaft of the engine to another pulley on the rear wheel. If the contraption had lights, they were likely powered by kerosene and turned on with matches or maybe a very rudimentary battery on more advanced models. A modern motorcycle has more computer chips than an early motorcycle had total moving parts.

Motorcycles weren't that much more complicated when I started riding. There had been a few improvements, but not many. Instead of total-loss electrical systems with enormous lead-acid batteries, the first motorcycles I rode had extremely basic six-volt electrical systems. These didn't provide enough juice to reliably power an electric starter, so we still had to kick-start our motorcycles. By then motorcycles had recirculating oiling systems so the rider no longer had to pump oil into the engine by hand, and chains took care of final drive duties instead of the smooth leather belts that spun the wheels on the earliest motorcycles, but overall, the bikes I started riding were closer to the motorized bicycles from the end of the nineteenth century than they were to the reliable, practical motorcycles we have today.

PUTTING THE MOTOR IN THE CYCLE

IN THIS BOOK I'M not going to teach you how to overhaul your motorcycle. Most modern motorcycles are too complicated for you to do much more than change the oil yourself, but you will need to become familiar with the essential parts of a motorcycle and how everything works together. If you already know these things, you might want to skip ahead to the next section, though it can never hurt to brush up.

The engine, of course, is what puts the *motor* in *motor*cycle. Engines come in two basic types: four-stroke and two-stroke. Two-stroke engines haven't been used much in the United States over the past several decades because of emissions standards. They're called "two-strokes" because every two strokes of the piston comprise one complete cycle. The piston goes down and draws in the fuel charge; it goes back up and fires the fuel charge. Two-strokes are simple engines that don't have internal oil-lubrication systems. Some of the oil lubricates the inside of the engine, and the rest is burned with the exhaust, which is why they pollute so much. The last full-sized street-legal two-stroke motorcycle sold in the U.S. market was Yamaha's RZ350 from the mid-1980s.

For several decades two-stroke engines dominated Grand Prix motorcycle racing because the engines are light and generate twice as many power pulses as a four-stroke engine, but they've been phased out over the past decade. In 2002 the top class switched from 500-cc two-strokes to 990-cc four-strokes, and in 2009 the 250-cc two-stroke class was retired, to be replaced by a 600-cc four-stroke class for the 2010 season. That leaves just the 125-cc class as the last of the two-stroke road racers.

But because two-stroke street bikes are too old and too small to be used as practical transportation, we won't be discussing two-strokes in this book. The day may come when we'll ride around on electric motorcycles powered by hydrogen fuel cells, but for the foreseeable future we'll be riding motorcycles powered by four-stroke gasoline engines.

The basic systems of a four-stroke engine are the bottom end, the cylinder block, the piston, the cylinder, the combustion chamber, the cylinder head, and the fuel intake system.

The Crankcase

The crankcase is often referred to as the "bottom end" because it's located at the bottom of almost every engine (though it's at the center of opposed engines like those found on a BMW twin or a four- or six-cylinder Gold Wing—I'll explain that later in this chapter). It consists of a crankshaft that rotates in a series of bearings. This rotation carries through the clutch, transmission, and final drive system, until it becomes the rotation of your rear tire on the pavement, which is what makes your motorcycle move down the road. Piston rods connect the crankshaft to the pistons.

These days most motorcycles are so reliable that if you regularly change your engine oil, you can ride for hundreds of thousands of miles and not give any thought to the bottom end, but that wasn't always the case. Before we had the advanced oils, oiling systems, and bearing materials we have today, spinning a bearing or throwing a rod was a common occurrence. These are catastrophic failures that can result in internal parts of the engine exploding through cases and cylinder barrels and becoming external parts. This can be a little like a grenade going off between your legs, so it's a very good thing that modern bikes have such reliable bottom ends.

To be fair, some of the methods we used to rely

on for hot-rodding our engines, like "stroking" them (this refers to the practice of installing a different crankshaft that increases the length a piston travels up and down in the cylinder, effectively increasing cubic inches without making the cylinder itself any larger), improved performance, but they also put more stress on the parts and increased the likelihood that the engine would grenade between a rider's legs. Modern motorcycle engines are too complex to easily stroke, though a few people still do this to their older 74-inch Shovelheads and Panheads. If you plan to do this to your engine, make sure you or whomever you hire to do the job knows what he's doing.

The Cylinder Block(s)

Every gas-piston engine has one or more cylinder blocks. They are aluminum blocks (any practical modern motorcycle that you will consider buying will have an aluminum engine) with a hole or holes drilled in it or them for the piston or pistons. This hole is usually lined with a steel liner for durability, though some motorcycles have cylinder walls coated with harder alloys in place of steel liners.

On a single-cylinder or an inline engine like that found on a four-cylinder sport bike or a parallel-twin engine like that found on a Triumph, there will be just one cylinder block. There are a small number of V-four engines in production; these usually have one large cylinder block with four holes drilled in it.

On a V-twin like a Victory or a Harley, there are two cylinder blocks. V-twin owners usually call these cylinder blocks "barrels" or "jugs" because they look like water barrels or jugs. They may have earned the name "jugs" because some people think they look a little like certain parts of a well-endowed woman, but it takes a lot of imagination to see the resemblance.

All motorcycle cylinder blocks (except a few specialized cylinder blocks used to build drag-racing engines) will feature some sort of cooling system. On water-cooled bikes this will consist of water jackets around the cylinders (hollowed-out spaces through which cooling water circulates from the radiator to the cylinder block and back to the radiator again). On air-cooled bikes like Harleys and Victories this will just be a series of cooling fins that provide a surface area over which the passing air can remove the heat generated from the combustion process.

The type of cooling system is probably the single most important factor in reliability and longevity in a modern engine. Liquid cooling is generally the best type when it comes to making an engine last. All modern cars and trucks are liquid cooled, and most modern engines will run for more than two hundred thousand miles.

Today's motorcycles are also water cooled, though air cooling is not necessarily a bad thing. As engine size increases, the amount of heat generated also increases, so it becomes harder to cool an engine with air alone when the cubic inches start to rise. As their air-cooled engines have grown larger, Harleys have had some cooling issues in recent years. To alleviate the problem Harley offers a system in which the rear cylinder shuts down at idle to help keep it cool when the bike is at rest.

Victory takes a different route. There are oil jets

in a Victory engine that spray streams of cooling oil at the bottoms of the pistons, right at the area in which the most heat is generated. The cylinders still crank out a hellacious amount of heat and will bake your inner thigh on a hot Arizona day, but that is true of just about every motorcycle. If you want to ride in air-conditioned comfort, you're reading the wrong book. I can tell you from tens of thousands of miles of experience that Victory engines seem to run cooler in stop-and-go traffic than Harley engines, which is one of the things I like about Victory motorcycles.

Harley does make what seems like a very good liquid-cooled motorcycle: the V-Rod. I have friends who own them and they speak very highly of them.

The Pistons, Cylinder, Combustion Chamber, Cylinder Head, and Fuel Intake System

The pistons—the aluminum slugs that go up and down in the cylinder blocks—are the beating heart of a motorcycle engine. They're powered by a fuel-air charge that burns in the combustion chamber, which is the area at the top of the cylinder. This burning generates an engine's energy as well as most of its heat.

The cylinder head is the assembly that sits atop the cylinder block. It contains valves that open and close to allow the fuel charge to get in and the spent exhaust gases to get out. Motorcycle engines can have anywhere from two to five valves per cylinder. Most Harleys have two valves per cylinder: one intake and one exhaust. Victory motorcycles all have four valves: two intake valves and two exhaust valves.

Some Hondas have three valves per cylinder, and a handful of Yamahas had five valves per cylinder, but most modern motorcycles will have four valves per cylinder.

With very few exceptions, the fuel-air charge is injected by electronically controlled atomizers on modern motorcycles, though there are still a few good used bikes out there that have old-fashioned carburetors mixing the fuel-air charge and getting it into the combustion chamber. Triumph recently switched from carburetion to fuel injection on its Bonneville-series twins, and these bikes had been some of the last new models to feature carburetors.

THE FOUR STROKES OF A FOUR-STROKE

FOUR-STROKE ENGINES ARE CALLED four-strokes because each cycle of the combustion process consists of four strokes of the piston. The first (downward) stroke is called the "intake stroke" because the intake valves open on this stroke and the downward-moving piston draws in the fuel-and-air charge. The second (upward) stroke is called the "compression stroke" because the upward-moving piston compresses the fuel-air charge, which is ignited very near the top of the compression stroke (called "top dead center," or TDC). The energy generated by this ignition is called "combustion," and it's what gives its name to the third (downward) stroke, the combustion stroke (also called the "power stroke"). The fourth (upward) stroke is called the "exhaust stroke" because the exhaust valves open on this stroke, allowing the upward-moving piston to force the spent exhaust gases out through the open valves.

REDLINING

I'M NOT A HUGE fan of Harley-Davidson motorcycles. That is partly because for many years Harley sold motorcycles that were worn-out antiques even when they were new. In 1969 AMF (American Machinery and Foundry) bought Harley. By that time the Japanese had begun to introduce motorcycles with modern technology, and in the following years the pace of development of motorcycle technology quickened. When AMF sold Harley in 1981, the motorcycles coming from Japan were so highly developed that they made the motorcycles they produced in the 1960s look like antiques.

The bikes Harley built between 1969 and 1981 had barely changed; if anything, they got even worse. AMF looked at Harley as a cash cow and milked it dry. The company put very little money into product development. Instead, AMF ramped up production so that besides selling antiquated motorcycles, Harley's quality control went down the toilet; not only were Harley's motorcycles handicapped with old-fashioned technology like cast-iron engines, but they also became increasingly unreliable.

It wasn't that way when I started riding. In the 1950s all but the most expensive high-performance motorcycles had cast-iron engines and Harleys were as good as or better than any other bike on the market. But within fifteen years the Japanese, German, and

Italian manufacturers were selling motorcycles with aluminum cylinder blocks almost exclusively. Besides Harley, only the British still used cast iron for their cylinder blocks, and it didn't work out too well for them: by the early 1980s the entire British motorcycle industry had gone bankrupt. In fact, the British motorcycle industry would have gone out of business many years earlier if the UK government hadn't propped it up for the last twenty years of its existence.

Harley almost died at the same time. The Motor Company continued to build bikes with cast-iron cylinder jugs until the mid-1980s, when the aluminum Evolution engine hit the market. Because it is important to me as a patriot to ride an American motorcycle, I was stuck riding unreliable cast-iron Shovelheads all those years, and they were terrible motorcycles. Back then I spent as much time wrenching as riding, and it pissed me off. Harleys got a lot better after they started building the Evolution engines, but even today they are still old-fashioned air-cooled pushrod engines. (That means they have their cams down in the bottom end, and they use pushrods to operate the valves.)

Only a few other motorcycle manufacturers still use pushrods, like Royal Enfield from India, Moto Guzzi from Italy, and Ural from Russia, none of which are terribly reliable motorcycles. I wouldn't consider any of these brands when buying a motorcycle for practical transportation. Almost every motorcycle built today uses modern overhead-cam systems. Even most V-twin engines, like the engine found in my Victory, feature overhead cams.

Overhead-cam engines are more efficient and generate more power than pushrod engines, all else being equal, because they keep the valves under more direct control, allowing the engine to rev higher before valve float sets in. Valve float occurs when the cam pushes open the valve more rapidly than the valve spring can close it—it's a bad thing. If your bike is equipped with a tachometer, it will have a red zone marked on its face beginning at a certain rpm (revolutions per minute) range. The rpm range where the red zone begins is called the "redline," and is usually the engine speed at which valve float sets in. If you run your tach needle past the redline, you can destroy your engine.

Having an engine explode between your legs is not an experience I'd wish on my worst enemy. It's rare that a motorcycle engine will explode like a grenade, sending shrapnel outside the engine cases, but what happens when you spin a bearing or throw a rod can be just as deadly.

Usually you'll be going faster than you should be when this happens, which may well be why your engine explodes. You'll be riding along, enjoying the open road, and your engine will seize up. This in turn stops your rear tire from turning and it happens in less time than it takes for your heart to beat. If you're not covering your clutch (we'll discuss this in the advanced riding section of the book) and don't immediately pull in the clutch lever to disengage the rear wheel from the seized engine, you'll skid out of control and crash.

If your bike starts to skid sideways before you pull in the clutch, you'll have an even worse crash. When your tire is skidding, you lose all traction. When you pull in the clutch and the tire starts turning again, you'll regain traction. If your bike has started to skid to one side or the other, when you regain traction it will snap back in the opposite direction. This can easily happen with such force that it launches the entire motorcycle in the air. Of course you'll get launched with it. This is called "high-siding," and short of hitting a tree or a guardrail, it's about the worse kind of single-vehicle crash you can have on a motorcycle.

Overhead-cam engines have much higher redlines than do pushrod engines, which is why they produce more power, but that isn't the main reason I advise against buying most of the bikes that use pushrods. During normal street driving you seldom get anywhere near the engine's redline; the problem is that most of the engines that use pushrods use other outdated technology, too, which is why pushrod engines tend to be less reliable than those with overhead cams.

ENGINE TYPES

THERE ARE AS MANY different types of four-stroke motorcycle engines as there are types of motorcycles. Several basic engine configurations exist, and unless you plan to drop a fortune buying some rare, exotic machine, the bike you end up with will feature an engine in one of the following configurations:

- Single Cylinder
- V-Twin

- Parallel Twin
- L-Twin
- Opposed Twin
- Inline Triple
- Inline Four
- V-Four
- Opposed Four
- Opposed Six

There are a few oddball designs other than these, but without exception they will either be antiques, or they will be rare (and expensive) exotics, both of which are better suited to collections sitting in museums than they are for useful transportation because the spare parts needed to keep them on the road will be virtually unobtainable.

For example, over the years there have been a handful of motorcycles built with V-8 engines, like the racing bikes Moto Guzzi made in the mid-1950s. Over the years a few other manufacturers have built V-8-powered motorcycles, but not many. Italian Giancarlo Morbidelli developed a V-8 sport bike in the mid-1990s, but at a price tag of $60,000, he only sold four of them. A company called Boss Hoss makes gigantic motorcycles powered by automotive-type V-8 engines, but these bikes are so huge that they are just novelties even for experienced riders. They're expensive novelties, too, starting at around $40,000 for a base model and climbing well past the $50,000 mark if you start adding accessories; most owners then end up dropping another $20,000 converting them to trikes because they are so huge that they're miserable to ride.

There have been a few other oddball designs, like the inline six-cylinder bikes built by Honda and Benelli in the 1970s and early 1980s, but these weren't the most practical motorcycles even when they were new. The odds that you will end up with a bike that uses an engine configuration not on the preceding list are too small to measure.

Single Cylinders

The most basic type of engine, and the earliest to be mounted on a two-wheeled machine, is the single cylinder. As the name implies, this is an engine with a lone cylinder. These engines have always been mounted in a motorcycle frame with the engine aligned with the wheels; the engine has been angled anywhere from a slight lean toward the rear wheel, as on the very earliest Indians from 1901, to a complete forward lean, with the cylinder laying flat, parallel to the ground, its top end pointed at the front wheel, as on a Honda Trail 70 or a Harley Sprint or a Moto Guzzi from the 1960s.

Today most of the single-cylinder bikes available are designed for riding off-road. People who ride off-road place more value on agility and light weight than they do on overall power output. Anyone who's ever had to pick up a fallen motorcycle on a rough dirt trail will understand the reason for this. Because of the nature of off-road riding, where you'll find yourself negotiating steep, narrow trails covered with boulders and logs and maybe even the remains of Jimmy Hoffa if you get far enough off the beaten path, off-road motorcycles tend to fall over on a regular basis. This is why the fenders, gas tanks, and many other parts of an off-road bike are made of soft, bendable plastic. The lighter and easier to maneuver a motorcycle is, the less likely you are to fall over in the first place, and the easier the bike will be to pick up when you inevitably do fall over.

There are a few single-cylinder street bikes on the market, too, but most of these are very small displacement machines, usually 250 cc and under. Although these may be adequate for some riders, they won't cut it for most bikers.

Suzuki has built a 650-cc cruiser-type bike for many, many years. The company used to call it a "Savage," which is ironic, given the bike's docile nature—it's about as savage as an angry Yorkshire terrier. In 2005 Suzuki renamed it the "S40," which probably stands for "single cylinder, 40 cubic inches." It's not a sexy name, but then it's not the most exciting motorcycle. The single-cylinder engine is on the gutless side, and it's far from a smooth-running machine—you won't be doing thousand-mile days on this thing—but it is adequate for a lot of people. You could consider this motorcycle the baseline for what constitutes an adequate motorcycle for full-sized adult people; anything smaller and less powerful will be too small and too underpowered for serious consideration.

V-Twins

The early single-cylinder engines didn't put out a lot of power; ratings of 3 or 4 horsepower weren't uncommon. To put that in perspective, the engine in the Suzuki S40, which I just called "gutless," puts out about 28 horsepower. Even at the beginning of the twentieth century, 3 horsepower was inadequate for most riders—these early bikes needed pedal-assist to produce enough power to climb even the smallest hill—so motorcycle manufacturers looked for ways to increase power output.

The quickest way to get more power is through more engine displacement. This has always been true, and it was especially true in the early years of motor-cycling because of the primitive engine technology of the day. Riders needed bigger engines, but the tech-nological limitations of the day prohibited engineers from simply enlarging the early single-cylinder en-gines. These limitations still exist, to some degree. If engineers make engines with bores that are too large, they run into breathing and combustion problems; if they make the strokes too long, they run into prob-lems with piston speeds.

Given that cylinders could only get so big, the obvious way to get more power was to use more cyl-inders. The very earliest multi-cylinder engines were V-twins—that is, engines with their cylinders ar-ranged in a V shape. This made a lot of sense at the time since motorcycles were still just motorized bi-cycles (which is why the pedal-assist system was still in place). A bicycle frame comes to a pronounced "V" at its base, right where the engine sat. Giving the engine a V shape made the engine fit the available space better.

Even though V-twins were the earliest type of multi-cylinder engines, they still have a lot to offer. In street bikes, they generally tend to be low-revving engines that produce large amounts of low-end torque.

Twisting Force

In the real world, torque means more than raw horsepower. Torque is the measurement of the twisting force generated by an engine. Since this twisting force is what twists the wheel around in circles and makes you move down the road, you feel torque a lot more than you feel raw horsepower.

This is where big V-twin engines like those found in Harleys and Victories perform well. A 600-cc sport bike like Yamaha's R6 produces a lot more power than Harley's latest 96-cubic-inch (1584-cc) engine: 112 horsepower for the Yamaha compared with 68 horsepower for the Harley.

If ultimate horsepower output was the only factor determining what motorcycle to ride, we'd all be riding Japanese sport bikes, but there's a lot more to picking out a good, all-around motorcycle than pure engine output. For a lot of people the 68 horsepower generated by a stock 96-inch Harley Twin-Cam is adequate as long as the torque output is sufficient.

The 2006 Yamaha R6 generates just 43 pound-feet of torque, while the 96-inch Harley V-twin cranks out about 77 pound-feet of torque and the V-twin in my Victory Vision produces 109 pound-feet of torque. That doesn't mean my Victory is faster; the Yamaha is so much faster that they are almost like two completely different vehicles. But to get speed from the Yamaha, you have to rev the engine way up past 10,000 rpm. In other words, to go fast, you pretty much have to ride it like you stole it, all the time. This is fun on a racetrack, if you know what you're doing, but out among the traffic found on real-world roads, it gets tiresome.

With a big V-twin like my Vision, peak torque is reached at just 2700 rpm. That means when I want to get access to my engine's twisting force, I don't have to shift down four gears, open up the throttle, and drive like a maniac. I just roll on the throttle and the power is instantly there. So while a sport bike like the Yamaha is a lot faster on a racetrack, a big V-twin like the Vision feels a lot faster in normal driving conditions on real-world roads.

There aren't many things in life I enjoy more than the feel of riding a motorcycle with a big, torque-rich engine. When I roll on the throttle, I feel an invisible hand pressing down on me. I feel like I'm part of the road, like I'm connected to the earth by something more than just the rubber of my tires.

L-Twins

Many people might argue that the L-twin engine design is really the same as a V-twin, and they would have a good argument. The L-twin is just a V-twin with the angle between the cylinders opened up to 90 degrees, so that the engine resembles an "L" rather than a "V."

The reason I broke this design out wasn't because I think it's a separate engine design; I did it because the L-twin is generally used in a different type of motorcycle. With a few exceptions, the V-twin engine tends to be used in large motorcycles designed for relaxed types of riding. The Italian companies Aprilia and Moto Guzzi make V-twin sport bikes in very low volume, as does the Austrian company KTM, and Honda and Suzuki have produced a number of V-twin sport bikes over the years, but for the most part V-twin engines power big touring bikes and cruisers.

That doesn't mean the V-twin engine doesn't have potential as a high-performance engine. For decades Ducati has built V-twin engines that have been winning world racing championships. But Ducati uses a 90-degree angle in its V-twin engines, with one cylinder laying flat, almost parallel to the ground, and the other almost upright, tilted back only slightly, so many people refer to these as L-twins.

Parallel Twins

Another early type of multi-cylinder engine was the parallel twin. This is an engine with its two pistons arranged side by side. The British company Triumph popularized this engine design. In 1937 Edward Turner developed the Speed Twin for Triumph basically by grafting two Triumph single-cylinder engines together in a side-by-side fashion. He was far from the first to build this type of engine, but Turner's 500-cc Speed Twin was the first commercially successful mass-produced British multi-cylinder motorcycle, and the basic design has defined the British motorcycle to this day.

When John Bloor resurrected the bankrupt Triumph in the late 1980s, he was determined to build modern, cutting-edge motorcycles rather than retro throwback twin-cylinder machines, but after more than a decade he finally relented, and in the early 2000s the company once again began building traditional parallel-twin motorcycles. Today Triumph's retro-styled twins are among its most popular machines.

There aren't a lot of parallel twins on the market today, but those that are available are decent, practical motorcycles. In addition to the Triumphs just mentioned, Kawasaki makes several mid-displacement parallel twins.

Opposed Twins, Fours, and Sixes

Another type of twin-cylinder engine that's been around almost as long as the motorcycle itself is the opposed twin. This is a two-cylinder engine with pistons that move outward, directly opposite from each other. Since a Harley has a 45-degree V-twin engine, a Ducati a 90-degree V-twin engine (an L-twin), you could almost think of the opposed twin as a V-twin with a 180-degree angle between the V, but if you follow that logic, you could consider a parallel twin a V-twin with a 360-degree angle (or a zero-degree angle, if you don't want to take the long way around), but this is, of course, nonsense.

Anyway, in an opposed twin, the pistons move outward, away from each other, then inward, toward each other. Early on someone figured this motion resembled the arms of a boxer, but any boxer who boxed with a motion like this would get his ass kicked regularly and severely. Regardless, the name stuck and opposed engines are called "boxers." Volkswagen used a boxer-type engine in its old air-cooled Beetles, and Porsche and Subaru continue to use boxer engines in their cars.

The boxer engine had been used in motorcycles for about as long as the V-twin. The design appeared as early as 1904 in what eventually became the Douglas motorcycle, and Harley developed the Model W Sport Twin, which featured an opposed-twin engine, in 1919, but it was Max Friz's use of the design in his R32, BMW's first motorcycle, produced in 1923, that made the engine design iconic. BMW continues to build motorcycles powered by opposed twins to this day, and it will probably continue to do so as long as motorcycles are still being built.

Even though BMW had a great deal of success with opposed-twin engines, no other manufacturer has mass-produced a motorcycle with such an engine since the end of World War II. It wasn't until Honda introduced its Gold Wing in 1975 that any major manufacturer built a motorcycle with a boxer-type engine, and Honda's version was a four cylinder rather than a twin. In 1988 Honda added two more cylinders to create the six-cylinder Gold Wing 1500. Then in 2001, Honda bumped displacement to 1832 cc.

Today BMW's R-series twins and Honda's GL1800 Gold Wing are the only bikes that use boxer engines, but these are extremely popular bikes and there are a lot of them on the road. This might be a relatively unusual engine design—and Gold Wings and BMWs are also expensive machines—but they are also some of the best and most-popular long-distance bikes you can buy. As I said earlier, for me it's important to buy motorcycles built by American companies, but you, like a lot of motorcyclists, might have different priorities; if you ride long enough and far enough, there's a good chance you could end up owning a bike with an opposed engine someday.

Inline Triples

Think of an inline three-cylinder engine as a parallel twin with one more cylinder tacked on. Inline triples have been used sporadically throughout the years. Right now the only company mass-producing inline triples is Triumph. The company builds a variety of triples ranging from 675-cc middleweights to the gigantic 2300-cc Rocket Three line. These are generally highly regarded bikes. Their three-cylinder engines do a good job of combining the low-end torque of twin-cylinder engines with the top-end rush of engines with more cylinders. Triumph has a long history with three-cylinder engines, dating to the 1960s.

Outside of Triumphs, you won't find a lot of triples to choose from. Some Italian companies may or may not build them, but that's the nature of an Italian motorcycle company. The Italians design some of the best motorcycles available, but when it comes down to actually building them, they seem to lose interest. As a result, Italian motorcycle companies are almost always in some state of receivership, what we'd call "bankruptcy" in the United States.

Because of this, I suggest staying away from Italian motorcycles. Period. You may be tempted by their beautiful styling or their high performance, but if you succumb to temptation and buy one, consider yourself warned, because you will, without exception, have all kinds of problems with your bike, ranging from untraceable electrical problems to camshafts that disintegrate within ten thousand miles.

This is in part because of communication problems in Italian motorcycle factories. Most of the managers in Italians factories are Italians who speak Italian, while most of the workers have emigrated from Africa or the Middle East and speak other languages. In other words, the workers don't understand a word their bosses are saying. As a result, bikes are shipped with huge problems. For example, a batch of camshafts won't have the proper heat treatment on the cam lobe surfaces, or an entire production run of bikes will be shipped with the wrong central processing units (CPUs) in their fuel-injection computers.

A big part of the problem is Italy's socialist government. This is not a book about politics, but the Italian motorcycle industry is an example of politics manifesting themselves in your motorcycle riding experience, so I think it deserves a mention here. In Italy, labor laws have been heavily influenced by the Communist Party. As a result, it's almost impossible to fire someone, regardless of how poorly that person performs. Thus, people tend to rise to their level of incompetence and stay stuck in that position until they retire.

Ultimately you end up with factories filled with incompetent craftsmen who build bikes with unreliable camshafts and incorrect ignition systems. In the early 2000s Italy hired Professor Marco Biagi to propose reforms to the country's labor laws that were intended to make Italy more competitive in world markets, but in March 2002, the Red Brigade, a radical Communist faction, had the professor killed, thus ensuring that Italy would continue building unreliable motorcycles for the foreseeable future.

Professor Biagi's tragic fate illustrates the immense barriers to reform. As a result, we're unlikely to see, in our lifetime, Italian industry adopt sensible labor laws—or produce reliable motorcycles. Until that happens, you are advised to stay away from anything Italian that has electrical parts. If you must buy Italian, it's best to stick to their guns and shoes, both of which still seem to be fairly reliable.

Inline Fours

In the 1960s Harley and Triumph continued to build motorcycles that still featured the technology they'd introduced in the 1930s, primarily because they could get away with it. They had virtually no competition in the heavyweight motorcycle market, so they had little reason to spend the money needed to update their products.

But if they had been paying attention, they would have realized that the lack of competition was an illusion; they had plenty of competition, and almost all of it was coming from Japan. When Honda began exporting motorcycles to the United States in 1959, its early bikes were little 50-cc step-through machines that resembled nothing so much as an old-fashioned girl's bicycle. These were soon followed by larger motorcycles with parallel-twin engines, but the biggest of these displaced just 305 cc; none of these engines were considered direct competitors with Triumph's 650-cc parallel twins and Harley's 900-cc and 1200-cc V-twins.

When Honda introduced its first "big" bike, the Black Bomber, a sporty 450-cc parallel twin, it should have sounded like a shot across the bow of the American and British motorcycle industries. Sure, it was only a 450-cc bike, but it could outrun the bigger British twins and could even give the mighty 900-cc Sportster a run for its money. And the Japanese had no intention of stopping there.

The British sort of got with the program. Triumph and BSA began developing three-cylinder motorcycles, but they more or less backed into the program with little enthusiasm. The resulting motorcycles, introduced in 1969, were half-assed at best, weak responses to the next bomb Japan was about to drop on the motorcycling world: the Honda CB750.

The CB750 had all the attributes that people had grown to associate with Honda: modern design (the CB750 featured an all-aluminum engine with an overhead camshaft), convenience (the CB750 featured an electric starter that worked every time the owner punched a button), and reliability—you could ride this bike from coast to coast without doing anything other than oiling and tightening the chain. But the most amazing aspect of the bike was its number of cylinders: four of them, all placed transversely in a row across the frame, like two side-by-side parallel twins.

There had been four-cylinder bikes in the past. In the early years Henderson and other companies had built motorcycles with longitudinal four cylinders—that is, the four cylinders were placed end to end, leading to a very long, awkward motorcycle. Because of this, and also because of their complexity, which made early fours even more unreliable than early twins and singles, the longitudinal four was never very popular. In the 1960s the Italian company MV Agusta built a relatively modern 600-cc transverse four, but in true Italian fashion it imported only twenty or thirty of its four-cylinder bikes into the U.S. market over the course of a dozen or so years. Odds are you'll never see one of these except on the pages of a magazine.

Honda was the opposite of an Italian company; whereas there were very few Italian motorcycle dealers in the United States in the 1960s and 1970s, by 1969 there was a Honda dealership in just about every town with more than a thousand people living in it. Unlike exotic Italian motorcycles, Honda's CB750 was everywhere, virtually overnight. And unlike the earlier 450 twin, which could almost keep up with the Sportster, Harley's fastest motorcycle at the time, the new 750 four, beat the Sportster like the Sportster owed it money. Harley responded by boring the Sportster out to 1000 cc, but this only made the marginally unreliable Sportster extremely unreliable. As a response to the CB750, the upsized Sportster was beyond pathetic.

The Japanese were far from done having their way with the rest of the world's motorcycle manufacturers. Honda's CB750 dominated the heavyweight motorcycle market for three years, driving more nails in the British motorcycle industry's coffin. Then in 1972 Kawasaki introduced the Z1, a 903-cc four cylinder with not one but two overhead camshafts. Not only could the Kawasaki smoke every British and American motorcycle (and also the CB750), it could hand the fastest cars their asses.

Soon all the Japanese manufacturers were producing motorcycles with bigger and faster inline four-cylinder engines. The engine design became so common that motorcycles with inline fours were called UJMs (universal Japanese motorcycles).

It's not hard to see why they became so popular. In 1973 a rider could plunk down $1,900 for a brand-new Z1 (hundreds of dollars less than a comparable Harley) and ride off with the fastest machine available to the general public. As a result, Kawasaki sold about 85,000 Z1s in 1973, while Harley sold just 9,875 XL 1000s (in 1973 Harley dropped the "Sportster" name and didn't reinstate it until the late 1970s). This trend would continue well into the next decade, nearly bankrupting Harley-Davidson in the process.

V-Fours

The last common type of motorcycle engine is the V-four. Honda introduced the modern V-four in the 1980s and now has two bikes available with the engine design: the ST1300 sport-tourer (we'll get into types of motorcycles in the next chapter) and the Interceptor, an 800-cc sport-tourer. Think of the V-four as an automotive V-eight sliced in half.

This design has advantages in packaging because it crams four cylinders into a unit that doesn't take up much more space than your average V-twin, but it's expensive to produce because it has a lot more individual parts than an inline four. Because of high production costs not many manufacturers build V-four production bikes today. Yamaha puts V-fours in a few of its Star-series cruisers, and Aprilia recently released a V-four sport bike, but the design has never caught on like the inline four and the V-twin.

FINAL DRIVE ASSEMBLY

WE'VE SPENT A LOT of time discussing engine designs, which makes sense since without motors we'd just have bicycles, but the rest of the parts are almost as important. For example, without a final drive assembly connecting the engine to the rear wheel, the motor would just be a noisemaking device.

Power can be transferred from the transmission to the rear wheel by three main methods: belt, chain, and shaft. The earliest motorcycles used a smooth leather belt to transmit power from a pulley coming straight off the engine's crankshaft to the rear wheel. Rather than a clutch and gear set, the transmission consisted of an idler pulley that put tension on the belt. This idler pulley was disengaged with a lever, a crude system that made harnessing the 2–3 horsepower that the early motorcycle engines put out a lot more exciting than you might imagine.

By the time I started riding, belts had long been abandoned in favor of chain final drive systems in which a metal chain ran from a sprocket on the output shaft on the transmission to another sprocket attached to the rear wheel hub. This system is still used on many bikes today.

Although most U.S. motorcycle builders progressed from belt final drive to chain final drive, a lot of European manufacturers developed shaft final drive systems. These systems don't require the periodic maintenance that chain systems require, such as tightening of the chain and constant lubrication, but they are heavy and add a lot of weight to the bike.

They also have a tendency to jack the bike up under acceleration. This unsettles the chassis and has a negative impact on handling. Some manufacturers like BMW and Moto Guzzi have developed complex rear suspension designs that help minimize this tendency, but these designs bring on a new set of problems. BMW in particular has had a lot of trouble with the failure of the articulating joints it puts in its drive shafts to help control the up-and-down jacking inherent in a shaft rear-drive system.

Harley-Davidson brought back the belt concept in the early 1980s, using a toothed rubber belt on toothed sprockets in place of the chain. The system runs as smoothly as a chain system, and a quarter of a century of use has proven it to be as reliable and easy to maintain as a shaft system. It was a great idea, as evidenced by the fact that today many other manufacturers use belt final drive systems on their motorcycles, including Victory, Yamaha, and BMW.

ELECTRICAL SYSTEMS

THE OTHER MAIN PARTS of a motorcycle are its frame, electrical system, transmission, and rider controls and accommodations. The frame, that part that holds the whole thing together, is made either of steel tubes or aluminum beams. In the old days we had to worry about the engine shaking frame welds and joints loose, but today's frames are so sturdy that this has become another forget-about-it part.

There are a few exceptions—for example, in the late 1990s Suzuki built the TL1000, a V-twin sport bike that developed a reputation for breaking frames—but as long as you're not regularly popping wheelies or doing gigantic stoppies (hitting the brakes so hard you raise your back wheel in the air), you're most likely not going to have to worry about problems with your motorcycle's frame.

In the old days the electrical systems of our motorcycles were constant sources of problems. One of the improvements the Japanese brought to the motorcycle industry was the concept of reliable electrical systems. These reliable electrics in turn made electric starters a practical proposition, which is what made it possible for so many new riders to get into the sport of motorcycling. This is especially true for women; it took a hefty leg to kick-start those old V-twin Harleys. The British never did quite get the hang of reliable electrical systems and electric-starters, which was still another nail in the British motorcycle industry's coffin, but Harley did make huge improvements and today's big Harley V-twins all have functional electric starters.

With maybe the exception of the Italian motorcycles, which still seem to have lots of electrical problems, most bikes sold today have reliable electrical systems and this shouldn't be something you have to worry about unless you hook up too many electrical accessories like heated seats, grips, vests, or driving lights. You will have to keep your battery charged, but this isn't that hard to do. If you ride every day, your battery should last for years. Even if your bike sits for weeks at a time, you can hook up a trickle charger that will keep your battery charged while waiting for you to go for a ride.

TRANSMISSIONS

MODERN TRANSMISSIONS ARE ANOTHER part of the motorcycle that don't warrant a lot of owner attention. With the exception of some Yamaha models, most modern motorcycle transmissions are as reliable as most automotive transmissions (I'll discuss Yamaha's past transmission problems in the section on buying used motorcycles).

Most motorcycles use six-speed or five-speed manual transmissions. A few bikes use automatic transmissions, but these are still controversial and haven't been widely accepted. The odds are one thousand to one that you'll end up with a manually shifted motorcycle with a hand-operated clutch and a foot-operated shifter. If you're used to automatic transmissions in your car, don't worry—shifting a motorcycle is a lot easier than it sounds. I'll discuss that in the section on operating your motorcycle.

SADDLES

OTHER THAN THE ENGINE, which dictates the character of a motorcycle, the system that will most affect you as a rider will be the controls and accommodations. When you start riding, you might not realize what kinds of seats, seating positions, and control arrangements best suit your body because you'll be so focused on mastering your riding skills that you won't give comfort much thought. As your riding skills develop, however, and you start to put longer and longer days in the saddle, comfort will become a much higher priority. Nothing takes the fun out of a long day of riding like an uncomfortable seat.

You might guess that the saddle is the single most important factor in being comfortable, and in a way it is—if your butt is burning, the rest of you is going to be damned uncomfortable, too. Most stock saddles are garbage, designed to provide the lowest possible manufacturing cost rather than maximum comfort. There are quality aftermarket saddles available from a variety of sources that will keep you comfortable for many hours after the stock saddle has given up all hope of supporting your ass. In my experience, Corbin makes the best seat available—I've ridden on them for almost twenty years.

WIND PROTECTION

THE SADDLE IS THE most obvious item that contributes to your comfort on a bike, but wind protection plays a big part, too. A lot of people like riding on motorcycles without fairings (the plastic bodywork that protects the rider from the wind) or windshields, and you might, too, but I like to have some wind protection. I switched to touring bikes with full weather protection in 1983. I had to start using fairings at that time because I had throat cancer and after a laryngectomy (surgery that left me breathing through a hole in my neck) the wind shear made it impossible for me to breathe, but I'm glad I switched to touring bikes. I feel a lot less tired after a long day in the saddle when I've been on a bike with a windshield or fairing.

I prefer a tall windshield, but some people don't like having to look through them. People who wear full-face helmets sometimes don't mind the wind flowing past their heads, as long as it doesn't knock their heads around. They consider a well-designed windshield or a fairing one they can look over, and not through, one that directs a clean, nonturbulent flow of air over and around their helmets. Klock Werks makes a windshield called the Flare for Harley baggers (touring motorcycles with saddlebags) that does a great job of smoothing out the airflow.

RIDING POSITION

WHEN YOU START RIDING, you'll probably be more concerned with how you look on your bike than how you feel on it. I don't really give two shits about how you look on your bike. Ape hangers (a tall handlebar that makes you reach for the sky to put your hands on the controls) might look cool, but they put a lot of pressure on your lower back and turn you into a giant sail to catch the wind.

The same goes for forward-mounted foot controls; you may look cool as ice leaned back in your saddle, your feet kicked way out in front of you like you were sitting in your La-Z-Boy recliner, but you'll be using your lower back to fight the wind the entire time you're on the road.

The sad fact is that most of us aren't that pretty to start with. I know I'm not. The way I see it, most of us are never going to look like movie stars on our bikes, no matter how uncomfortable we make ourselves; we might as well be comfortable.

Motorcycles are a lot more complex than they might seem at first glance, but you really need to keep only the following few things in mind.

WHAT YOU SHOULD KNOW

- The engine gives the motorcycle its character.
- Horsepower might win races, but on the street torque is king.
- The more comfortable your bike, the more you enjoy riding.

CHAPTER TWO

TYPES OF BIKES
What to Ride

My goal is to make you a lifelong motorcyclist. You'll need to do a lot more than just buy a $20,000 Harley—you'll need to devote yourself to not only learning to ride, but also learning to appreciate the ride. You'll know you've become a serious motorcyclist when you don't ride just because your buddies are taking their bikes out together; you ride because you can't wait to feel the freedom of the open road. Hell, you won't ride because you want to ride; you'll ride because you *need* to ride.

To get to that point, you need to rack up many miles in the saddle, and having a comfortable motorcycle makes putting in those hours a lot more fun. This is something you should keep in mind from the very beginning, when you first start thinking about getting a motorcycle. There's a lot more to being comfortable on your bike than just saddles, handlebars, and windshields. The type of bike you choose will go a long way to determining how at ease you become on your bike.

If you're just starting out, it's easy to be confused by all the different kinds of motorcycles on the market. And even if you've been riding awhile, you may have picked a bike that's not the right bike for you, and now you're stuck with a machine that doesn't meet your needs.

When it comes to picking a bike, in the end it boils down to what you like. You need guts to ride the bikes you like the best. You should decide what's important to you and then pick the best bike that meets your requirements. Don't choose a motorcycle to impress other people; choose one that impresses you. *Don't worry about what other people think.* Instead, decide what bike's best for you, then get out there and have fun on it.

I pick my bikes based on my own priorities. As I've mentioned, it's important to me to ride an American bike. I have always ridden American, which is why I stuck with Harley-Davidson until Victory's bikes came along. I feel that way about everything. I ride an American-bred quarter horse, and I drive an American pickup (a Chevy). I grew up during World War II and was taught to buy *only* American.

It hasn't always been easy to ride American. I've never liked Harleys much—I've always considered them to be the bottom of the technology pile—but I rode Harleys for fifty-two years because they were the best American bikes. Today I ride a Victory Vision because I think that's the finest bike America makes. There are so many good motorcycles to pick from today that it's hard to judge them all, but I've ridden enough to know that my Victory stacks up well against any of them.

In this section I'm going to help you figure out what's important to you when it comes to your bike. We're going to look at the types of motorcycles out there and examine the advantages and the disadvantages of each. We're going to talk about the comfort, controllability, reliability, and convenience of each type of bike.

Once you understand all of this, you might find that the bike you intially thought you wanted is actually the wrong bike for you. You may think you want a big bagger but you might not be aware of the challenges of riding a bike that's physically too large for you to ride smoothly and controllably. And you might not be aware of the costs associated with a bagger. For instance, it'll cost you more to mount new tires on an Electra Glide or Gold Wing than you'll spend on maintenance in an entire year for a Sportster. And it costs a lot more to change tires on a crotch rocket than on a dual-sport machine. Once you know what types of motorcycles are out there, you'll be better able to understand the costs associated with each.

When I first started riding, there wasn't much variety from which to choose. One bike more or less served every purpose. You could buy a single-cylinder British bike like a BSA Gold Star and do everything with it, from commuting to racing. If you wanted to ride it off-road, you took off the lights and fenders and put on a set of dirt tires. With that setup, you could use it for trail riding, dirt-track racing, or hare scrambles, which are cross-country races. If you wanted to road race it, you could get a racing fairing, mount a set of road tires, and presto! You had a competitive road racer. And if you wanted to travel across the country, you just threw on a set of saddlebags and were set to hit the road. Beginning in the 1960s, motorcycles began to get more specialized. This trend has continued to the point that today many motorcycles are so narrowly focused they're only really good for doing one thing.

ON-ROAD VERSUS OFF-ROAD

PROBABLY THE MOST BASIC division between types of motorcycles is on-road versus off-road. I picked those categories instead of "dirt" versus "street" because by "off-road" I mean any motorcycle you can't license for use on public highways; this includes all racing motorcycles, whether those motorcycles are meant for racing on dirt or pavement. This book is a street-survival guide, and we're going to focus on motorcycles you can legally ride on the street.

Racing motorcycles, whether dirt bikes or road racers, are the most highly specialized motorcycles of all, and riding them requires specialized training and skills. Lots of good books and training schools are available for anyone interested in racing motorcycles, so we're not going to get into that here. We'll discuss riding on gravel and dirt roads when we get to riding techniques, and even talk about some mild trail riding, but it will be the type of riding you might be able to do on a street bike or a street-legal dual-purpose motorcycle.

The requirements for licensing a motorcycle to legally ride on the street vary from state to state, but the minimum requirements for a motorcycle to be street legal are usually that it has a functioning headlight, a taillight, a brake light, and often a horn. Most states also require turn signals on newer models.

That doesn't mean you can just take a race bike or a dirt bike, wire up some lights, and go get a license plate. Likewise you might run into problems if you try to license a custom-built motorcycle, or if you've bought a custom-built motorcycle from a builder. Almost every state requires a motorcycle to be manufactured specifically for use on public roads, meaning that it will pass all state and federal department of transportation and emissions requirements. Usually the licensing bureau can tell if your bike is legal just from the serial number.

Some people have figured out how to get license plates on just about anything, but I've never had any reason to do this. I always ride street-legal motorcycles, so I've never looked into what's involved. Besides, licensing a nonconforming motorcycle is illegal just about everywhere, and in some states doing so will even land you in jail.

I've got people from various law-enforcement agencies watching my every move so I can't get away with anything. The last thing I need is to end up in jail because I broke the law to get a license plate for a Harley XR750 dirt-tracker or some one-off chopper that doesn't meet state and federal regulations. The feds would probably say it was a larger conspiracy and charge me with racketeering. If you want to do this, that's your business, but you'll need to seek advice from someone else.

ANTIQUE MOTORCYCLES

You'll also have to learn about antique motorcycles elsewhere. This book is a guide for people who want to become hard-core motorcyclists, riders who want to get out on the road and put some serious miles under their butts. For that you're going to need a reliable modern motorcycle that doesn't break down or need extraordinary maintenance. That rules out antique or custom motorcycles.

Antique motorcycles have old parts that are often worn out and hard (or even impossible) to replace when they break out on the road. They just don't make this stuff anymore. This was true even before these bikes became antiques; back in the 1950s when we rode motorcycles built in the 1940s, it was nearly impossible to find replacement parts. Even if the antique motorcycle has been perfectly restored, you'll still be relying on an outdated electrical system. Most antique engines either use undependable six-volt systems or they have total-loss magneto systems, neither of which is conducive to having a motorcycle that starts every time you need it to start.

There is something kind of cool about kick-starting an old motorcycle. It requires skill to get an old bike running, but take it from me—it's a lot of work. Having a motorcycle that starts every time you push a button on your handlebar is very convenient. If a bike has a kick-starter, it's almost certainly an antique and is best suited for sitting in someone's collection, and not for getting you where you need to go.

Old bikes might be cool, but everything about modern motorcycles is better than old bikes, from a practical standpoint. Even the basic material from which manufacturers make engines has improved over time. Now engines are made out of aluminum instead of cast iron because aluminum cools better and thus doesn't wear out as fast.

Still, antique motorcycles are great to look at in shows. It's fun to see how motorcycle technology developed, and for some of us old-timers it's nostalgic to see the types of bikes we used to ride. But when it comes to getting from one place to the other safely and reliably, I wouldn't want to go back to the old days. Give me the most functional, reliable modern motorcycle available. Unless you are a wizard mechanic who can overhaul your bike by the side of the road with nothing but an adjustable wrench and a Zippo lighter, you're better off avoiding "classic" bikes as your main source of transportation.

CHOPPERS AND BOBBERS

I ALSO RECOMMEND STAYING away from custom motorcycles when you're starting out, for the same reason you should avoid antiques: they are complete pains in the ass to own and ride. Custom motorcycles are bikes that have been modified or even built from scratch. The most common are choppers and bobbers.

When I first started riding, if you said the word *motorcycle* in the United States, the first thing that came to mind was a big, heavy Harley-Davidson. At the time these were the best bikes available for comfortable highway riding, but a lot of us wanted more performance than a stock Harley was capable of delivering. We didn't have much money to buy parts to make the engines faster, and even if we did, such parts weren't easy to come by. We couldn't just go online, order whatever we wanted, and have it shipped across the country. More often than not if we wanted a specific part, we had to figure out a way to make it ourselves.

A cheaper and easier way to make our bikes faster was to take parts off and make them lighter. That didn't cost any money at all, so most of us younger guys chopped parts off to create stripped-down hot-rod bikes. We'd take off fenders, extra lights, any bodywork that wasn't absolutely necessary, and pretty much anything else that didn't contribute to making the bike faster. Some guys even took off the brakes!

We never really had a name for the bikes we customized. According to the stories you read in the press, people called this type of bike a "bobber" or a "bob job," because some people called taking off parts "bobbing" back then. They're still called "bobbers" today, but I think names like "bobber" and "chopper" came from the motorcycle industry and not the people out there customizing bikes. They probably figured it would be easier to sell us junk if they gave it a catchy name.

By the time the industry types started calling our custom bikes "choppers," we'd begun to focus more on style. This happened during a wild time in our country's history. A lot of craziness was happening, and we were young and a little wild ourselves. Our bikes reflected that. People started chopping and re-welding frames to increase the rake of the bike (the angle at which the fork extends away from the frame). They also made forks longer and handlebars higher. Every year people made their forks longer, their handlebars higher, and their rakes more extreme until it got so out of control that the bikes became just about impossible to ride.

Throughout all this insanity I kept my bikes pretty functional. I did some stuff that I now realize was probably crazy, like removing the front brakes and extending the front forks, though never by more than four inches. I also took the rocker-arm clutch pedal and cut it in half, turned it upside down, and made a suicide clutch out of it. With no front brake and a suicide clutch, I had to hit neutral at every stop. That's not the safest way to stop.

I never changed the rake on any of my bikes; a radically raked front end is one of the main characteristics of a chopper. Then, as now, I liked to ride more than anything. I like to move hard and fast, which is not what choppers are meant to do. Engineers spend years developing the best angle for a bike's rake, which largely determines how a bike handles. In the 1940s Harley tried a different rake on its bike each year, looking for the perfect angle, but the company never quite nailed it because the Harleys of the 1940s and even 1950s needed steering dampers to prevent high-speed wobbles. I don't think Harley really got it right until the 1960s, when it was able to do away with the steering damper.

If it took Harley decades to find the perfect angle for the rake of its bikes, I don't expect that I'd be able to improve a bike much by spending an afternoon cutting and welding my frame to get a different rake. I'm not an engineer, but neither are all the other people experimenting with the rakes on their custom bikes. As a result of all this backyard engineering, virtually every radically raked custom bike built during the 1960s and 1970s was unsafe to ride.

I've talked to custom bike builders today who claim that they've figured out the right measurements to make a radically raked custom bike safe to ride, and I imagine that they're a lot safer than earlier examples, but I have a hard time believing that these builders can make a bike handle as well as the engineers who design frames using decades of research on motorcycle handling.

Arlen Ness, the king of the customs, may be an exception. Arlen has been a very good friend of mine for over fifty years and probably knows as much about engineering a motorcycle chassis as anyone at any motorcycle-manufacturing company. His bikes handle better than any other custom I've ever ridden (and better than a lot of factory bikes), but I still ride a mostly stock motorcycle. When it comes to motorcycle riding, I have enough to worry about without having a bike that is trying to kill me because of its poorly engineered chassis. I want my motorcycle to be safe; just "safer" doesn't quite cut it.

Choppers and bobbers may look cool, but they're better to look at than they are to ride. Some people claim that their custom bikes are reliable, but I've been riding a long time with a lot of people, many of whom ride choppers and bobbers, and in my experience these types of bikes are anything but reliable. They're homemade bikes, and as such they're prone to all sorts of oddball failures that you never encounter on a well-engineered, mass-produced motorcycle.

The welds on homemade gas and oil tanks seldom seem to stand up to the constant shaking of V-twin engines, and custom bikes spring leaks with such regularity that you can almost count on this happening if you ride any farther than the local bar or café. Their electrical systems are usually homemade, too, and unless the guy who did the wiring was a certified genius, these bikes are more likely to short out and leave you stranded than they are to run reliably. In Arizona during April (when we have our annual bike week), almost every bike you see broken down on the side of the road is a custom that someone thought was reliable enough to ride a lot of miles. They thought wrong.

Even if these bikes were reliable enough to use for everyday transportation, they're too uncomfortable to ride for more than half-hour to forty-five-minute stretches. The riding position is designed to make you look cool rather than to make you comfortable. As a result, homemade bikes place you in the worst possible riding position for long days in the saddle.

After just a few hours, parts of you that you didn't even know you had will hurt. Your joints will hurt, your internal organs will hurt, and your muscles will feel like you've just spent an afternoon being pummeled by a boxer. Some people are into this, but then some people are into pouring hot wax on their privates. To each his own, I suppose, but pain doesn't do much for me.

Choppers are more uncomfortable than bobbers because a proper bobber will put you in a slight forward lean, taking a little pressure off your lower back. It will handle better, too, because a bobber doesn't have the long, kicked-out fork that a chopper has. Because of its traditionally shorter fork and relatively conservative rake, a bobber turns a lot tighter than does a long chopper. Even so, a bobber is still a homemade bike and as likely to suffer breakdowns and failures as any other homemade bike. Unless you're a skilled mechanic and have the patience to spend as much time working on your bike as you do riding it, I'd leave the custom bobbers and choppers to the Hollywood types who can afford to have a mechanic following them around with a complete set of tools and a spare bike.

MANAGING YOUR MACHINE

THE TYPE OF BIKE you choose for your first motorcycle could determine how well you're ever going to learn to ride. If you start out on a motorcycle that doesn't allow you to completely control it, it will control you. You'll develop bad habits for the rest of your riding career. Take, for example, my habit of putting a motorcycle in neutral when I come to a stop, even though I know this is an unsafe practice. I developed this habit early on and I can't shake it. If you develop enough of these bad habits when you first start riding, you won't control your own motorcycle. Instead, you'll be at its mercy.

The most important thing to look for in your first motorcycle is manageability. The biggest mistake people make when buying their first bike is to purchase a bike that's physically too big or too powerful for them to manage. Riding well is all about being in control of your machine, and when you start out with too much motorcycle, you'll never master it.

You'll want to get a ride that is small enough to control, but picking a first bike isn't as simple as getting the smallest motorcycle you can find. When I traded my first real bike, the 45-cubic-inch Indian Scout I mentioned earlier, for a Harley, I wanted to get a 45-cubic-inch Harley, but a friend talked me into getting a larger 61-cubic-inch Harley. It took a little practice to get used to the bigger bike, but after a few rides, when I was comfortable with it, I was thankful I hadn't gotten the smaller machine.

You shouldn't get a 1,000-pound bagger or a 1400-cc crotch rocket that can hit 200 miles per hour, but you also won't want an underpowered machine that isn't capable of keeping up with traffic or a motorcycle that's physically too small for you. You'll want a bike that is small enough for you to control, but one that is big enough for you to ride comfortably and has enough power so that you won't get bored with it too soon.

How small a motorcycle you need depends on how big you are. I have a friend named Tiny who's one big motorcycle rider. What constitutes a small motorcycle for him is a whole lot different from what constitutes a small motorcycle for a woman who stands five feet tall and weighs eighty pounds soaking wet.

When I started riding, there weren't a lot of options for beginner motorcycles. If you had a lot of money, you bought a Mustang, which was a very cool little minibike styled to look like a full-sized motorcycle. There were a few other options for a kid with too much money, but not many. Back then Harley made some small bikes based on a 125-cc two-stroke engine from German maker DKW. Harley got the tooling for that engine as part of Germany's wartime reparation. In 1948 Harley put the little two-stroke engine into the Model S, a fun little bike with a girder-type front suspension, rigid rear, and a little "peanut" tank that later turned up on the XLCH Sportster. A lot of kids must have had the $325 that Harley charged for the Model S because the company sold more than ten thousand of the little two-stroke machines.

If you didn't have a lot of money, you did what I did and bought a Cushman scooter. I was just a kid, about thirteen or fourteen years old, when I got my Cushman. At that time you could get a Cushman for $25 to $50. That was a lot of money for a kid like me, making just $7 per week working at a part-time job. I worked a lot of hours to earn the $25 I needed to buy the Cushman, but I didn't really have a choice because I knew I had to ride, even in my early teens.

HOW SMALL IS TOO SMALL?

GENERALLY SPEAKING, YOU SHOULD probably consider buying a 400-cc or larger motorcycle, even as your first bike. Some of the Japanese companies make street-legal motorcycles that are as small as 125 cc, but even if these bikes are capable of hitting a safe freeway speed, they'll likely be running at or near redline to do so. A 250-cc bike might hit 70 or even 80 miles per hour, but at that speed the engine will be revving so high that running at freeway speeds for an extended period will quickly wear out both the rider and the bike. That same bike might cruise comfortably at 60 miles per hour and be able to hold that speed all day long, but consider that traffic on metropolitan freeways often moves at 70 or 75 miles per hour, even when the posted limit is 55 or 65.

Although it might be technically illegal to ride at speeds five to ten miles per hour higher than the posted speed limit, it can be dangerous not to do so. Study after study has shown that what causes accidents is not speed itself, but rather disparities in speed. If you are moving at a different speed from the other vehicles on the road, whether you are going faster or slower, you are at much greater risk of having an accident than if you travel at the same speed as the other traffic, within reason. It might seem obvious that if you ride much faster than the other vehicles on the road you are at greater risk, but a less obvious fact is that you are at a much greater risk if you ride slower than other vehicles.

Think of traffic as a flowing stream of water. If the water is flowing unimpeded, its movement is almost invisible, but if you put an impediment like a rock or log in the stream, the moving water starts swirling in all kinds of chaotic directions. When you ride slower than the surrounding traffic is moving, you become that impediment, and the drivers swerving around you will continuously create potentially life-threatening situations for the duration of the trip.

RISING FATALITIES

IN RECENT YEARS, UNFORTUNATELY, there's been a tremendous increase in the number of motorcycle fatalities. In 2008 motorcycle fatalities increased for the eleventh year in a row. A lot of reasons account for this, notably the fact that in 2008 motorcycle registrations also increased for the eleventh year in a row. More motorcycles on the road mean more accidents. But that's not the whole story.

I blame at least part of the increase in motorcycle fatalities to the rise in cell-phone use. Recent studies have shown that drivers yapping on their cell phones are impaired even more than they would be if they were drunk. This means bikers have to concentrate even harder to prevent accidents. I always tell new riders, "It doesn't matter who is at fault in a collision with a car because you are the one who will get hurt."

Sometimes preventing accidents is impossible, but

some ways of preventing wrecks are in our control. For example, you always should avoid riding while drinking alcohol; even if you've just had a beer or two and don't feel like you have a buzz, your reaction times are slowed down enough to put you in danger. We can control whether or not we ride at the same speed as traffic, at least if our bikes are fast enough to keep up with the rest of the vehicles on the road. How fast that is depends on the road. If you live in a western state with lots of open space, traffic moves a lot faster than it does in the congested and heavily patrolled urban areas in the East. If you live in New Jersey or New York City, you might never need to go more than 70 miles per hour, but if you live in Aspen, Colorado, you may find traffic moving at 90 miles per hour on the freeway into Denver.

If you never leave a congested urban area and never ride on a freeway, you might be able to get by with a 250, but then you won't have the option of leaving town or using the freeway when you need to, and sooner or later that will happen. Even a 400- or a 450-cc motorcycle might be too small to be a practical bike for most people. Your best bet is to get a bike that's at least 500 cc to 650 cc to start. If you're a larger person, you might even consider something as big as a 1200 or 1300 for your first bike.

SPECIFIC TYPES OF MOTORCYCLES

As I MENTIONED EARLIER, motorcycles have evolved into highly specialized machines. Instead of that one BSA Gold Star that could do everything, we now have a wide variety of styles of motorcycles from which to choose, each one focused on doing just one thing well. The trick is to decide what you need your bike to do and select the type that best meets your needs.

The main types of street-legal motorcycles include the following:

- Dual Sport
- Supermotard
- Cruiser
- Touring Bike
- Sport-Tourer
- Sport Bike
- Standard

The first specialized motorcycles were purpose-built race bikes. Companies like Harley-Davidson and Indian engineered bikes purely for racing purposes even before World War I, but since race bikes have always been non-street-legal machines, we won't go into them here. Besides, purebred racing bikes weren't available to the general public then, and they're still hard to find (and very expensive).

Dual Sports
Off-road motorcycles were the first specialized bikes that were widely available. These began to show up in the 1960s. At first they were just street bikes with long-travel suspension and high pipes, but they became increasingly specialized and competition ready. Today you can buy a bike that's ready to

go motocross racing right off the showroom floor. Again, these were (and are) purely racing machines, but as they grew in popularity, manufacturers began to offer dual-purpose motorcycles that had some of the characteristics of these off-road racers in street-legal packages. Back when they first appeared, these were called "enduros," named after a type of mild off-road racing that was popular at the time. Today these are commonly called "dual sports."

Dual sports are usually dirt bikes that have been modified with lighting and emissions equipment that make them street legal. While dual sports are heavier than their dirt-only counterparts because of their additional equipment, they retain varying degrees of off-road capabilities. The most extreme examples—like the dual sports from KTM, Husqvarna, and some of the other European manufacturers—really are dirt bikes with headlights and oversized mufflers. They retain most of the off-road capabilities of their dirt-bike brethren.

Part of the reason dirt bikes perform well on dirt is because they have extremely long travel suspensions. A street-bike suspension only has to face potholes and the occasional road debris; in the worst instances, a street-bike shock or fork seldom has to compress more than a few inches. Dirt bikes have to cope with much greater impacts. Motocross and supercross racing has evolved into an extended series of high jumps, with the bikes flying twenty to thirty feet in the air; their shocks and forks compress a foot or more when the bikes land, so they need a lot more travel.

The extreme dual sports, the ones that are practically ready for off-road racing straight off the dealer floors, also have long-travel suspensions. This is great if you plan to do double and triple jumps with your motorcycle, but the drawback is that it makes the bikes ridiculously tall. Try climbing up on a KTM dual sport in a showroom sometime; just make sure you have someone beside you to catch you if you fall, because you'll be lucky if even the tips of your toes touch the showroom floor.

The extreme dual sports also have many of the same other drawbacks as dirt bikes, right down to the vinyl-covered fender protectors that pass for seats. Since dirt-bike racers usually stand when they ride, the seat, such as it is, exists mainly as a pad to keep the rider from bumping his or her ass on the fender. It was never designed as a place to sit. These dirt-bikes-with-lights are okay if you plan to do serious off-road riding, but they aren't great choices for practical street bikes.

The extreme examples aren't very useful for anyone but an off-road racer who has to ride his or her bike from trail to trail on public roads, but the bulk of dual-sport machines available today do make pretty good choices for first bikes, provided your legs are long enough to ride them comfortably— although they aren't as tall as the extreme versions, they're still tall enough to pose a problem for a lot of riders. Just throwing a leg over one can be a challenge if your inseam is less than thirty-two inches. Sitting that high gives you a commanding view of traffic, but if the seat is so high that you can't hold up the bike securely at a stoplight, the height can become a safety issue. I once had a vertically challenged rider fall onto me when he dropped his tall dual sport at a stoplight. He couldn't get his foot down securely and went tumbling over, almost taking me with him.

More reasonable dual sports usually range in size from 400 cc to 650 cc, and these have more than enough power to keep up with traffic. They are light, maneuverable, and generally inexpensive to buy, operate, and insure. Plus they're relatively simple so you can do most of the maintenance yourself if you have any mechanical experience at all; and if you do need to hire someone to work on them for you, the costs will be a lot less than for other types of bikes. Most of them have little or no bodywork that needs to be removed to change oil and tires or adjust valves, and because they only have one cylinder, they only have one set of valves to adjust. Since they have spoked wheels, most of them still use tube-type tires, making the repair of a flat tire a relatively inexpensive proposition, too.

If you have any interest in driving off the beaten path, if you don't mind not having the fastest and fanciest motorcycle around, and, most important, if your legs are long enough to safely ride a dual sport, then this type of bike might be right for you.

Supermotards

Supermotard bikes were developed for supermoto racing. This is a type of racing that is usually done in parking lots and can encompass sections of track that are both paved and dirt. The bikes themselves are usually created by taking dirt bikes and fitting them with street suspension and street tires. They look like dirt bikes with road-racing tires mounted on them.

Supermotards can be a lot of fun for an experienced rider, but only for short bursts of hooligan-type behavior. If you like to do wheelies and stoppies or big, smoky tire slides, few bikes do these things better than a supermotard.

But if you're looking for a practical all-around motorcycle, you'd do well to look at something other than supermotard bikes, because they are basically dirt bikes for the street, which means they're extremely uncomfortable to ride for any distance at all, mostly because they have dirt-bike-style seats. Add to this the fact that supermotards are generally expensive, costing as much or more than many full-sized motorcycles, and you can see why this type of bike is less than ideal for a beginner.

Cruisers

You'll most likely end up with a "cruiser," as the magazines call them. This is an odd name for a poorly defined style of motorcycle. The cruiser came into existence as a response to the custom bobbers and choppers we built in the 1950s and 1960s.

Up until roughly 1970 Harley only built two main types of big bikes: the XL Sportster and the FL Electra Glide. The Sportster was a hot rod back then, a lightweight high-performance bike. Remember, this was before Kawasaki started the Japanese horsepower wars with its 900-cc Z1 and right around the time Honda released its 750 four cylinder. Harley's other main line consisted of the big FL Electra Glide models. These were enormous 74-cubic-inch

(1200-cc) motorcycles loaded down with touring accessories. Most people considered these old men's motorcycles; we called them "garbage wagons" because of all the touring equipment on them.

Today I ride a full-dress motorcycle—you think differently when you are seventy than you did when you were eighteen—but we were young then. Because we young guys generally didn't want to ride around on the same types of bikes that our fathers and grandfathers rode, a lot of us customized our motorcycles. Some of us built full-on choppers and bobbers, but others just rearranged the basic material we already had available. Some guys rode stock Sportsters, but most of us preferred the smoother-running and more-reliable FL platform. Still, a lot of people wanted the cut-down look of the Sportster, so they got rid of the big, heavy Electra Glide fork with its chrome-plated steel covers and mounted the sleek, light fork from the Sportster.

The people running Harley-Davidson noticed what riders were doing to the machines they built and decided to cash in on it by offering a bike from the factory that resembled the machines people were building at home. In 1971 the Motor Company grafted a Sportster fork on an Electra Glide frame and created the Super Glide, an entirely new kind of motorcycle. I got my first Super Glide in 1972, and got my first Low Rider in 1977, after I got out of prison. It was great to have a bike that looked good right from the factory, but that didn't stop us from modifying them even more. Most of my modifications during these years were to improve a bike's performance. For example, I'd take the hydraulic disc brakes from Japanese bikes and mount them on a Harley.

The Super Glide caused a stir, and it wasn't long before other companies like Norton, Triumph, and then the Japanese companies—Yamaha, Honda, Kawasaki, and Suzuki—started offering bikes with similar style. People didn't know what to call this new type of bike, exactly. For a long time the magazines called them "customs," and later they started identifying them as "cruisers," which is the term most of the trade press still uses today. Some European magazines call them "soft choppers," which sounds even more foolish than "cruisers," so I guess we shouldn't complain.

For the most part, cruisers make good motorcycles for beginners. They are relatively light, compared with full-boat touring bikes. At the same time they are full-sized motorcycles with plenty of room for a rider and a passenger. Though they can sometimes put your arms and legs in awkward positions, cruisers are generally comfortable enough for the long haul, especially when fitted with good saddles and windshields. Plus most of them have tractable engines that help newer riders develop smooth throttle control.

Cruisers usually cost more than dual sports, but for most normal-sized people who do the vast majority of their riding on paved roads, they are more practical. You can get cruisers as small as 250 cc, but the smallest you should probably consider for a first bike is Kawasaki's 500-cc Vulcan. If you're a big person, or if you have some riding experience, you might consider getting something as large as the 100-cubic-inch (1634-cc) Victory Vegas. Some of the Japanese companies make cruisers that range up to 2000 cc, and Triumph makes one that displaces 2300 cc, but even a lot of experienced riders find bikes that displace more than 1700 cc to 1800 cc clumsy to ride.

If you're just starting out, you're better off getting a lighter, more manageable bike in the 500-cc to 1300-cc range. You can find a lot of nice cruiser-type motorcycles in this range, including Triumph's 865-cc America and Harley's Sportster line.

Touring Bikes

Unless you're an experienced rider, you'll want to stay away from the type of bike I ride, and have ridden for the past twenty-five-plus years: a touring bike. As I noted earlier, touring bikes—especially Harley-Davidsons—are often called baggers because one of their defining characteristics is the presence of saddlebags. On most touring bikes these are panniers mounted as a pair, one on each side of the rear wheel. Most often these will be made of some sort of plastic or fiberglass, but a lot of cruiser-based touring bikes have saddlebags made of leather or vinyl. The other features you'll usually find on touring bikes are fairings or windshields, comfortable saddles, and often some type of tail trunk. Most of the high-end touring bikes have all sorts of electronic gadgets, like stereos, CB radios, cruise control, and even heated seats and handgrips.

I have heated grips and a heated seat on my Victory Vision, but the feature I like best is the six-gallon gas tank, which lets me ride 200 to 250 miles without stopping to refuel. This lets me pile on lots of miles each day.

Telling you not to start out with a touring bike may sound like do-as-I-say-not-as-I-do type of advice, but touring bikes are extremely large motorcycles and a rider should have at least a few years under his or her belt before taking on one of these beasts. Victory claims a dry weight of 804 pounds for my Vision.

A lot of touring bikes are as heavy as or even heavier than my Vision. Honda's Gold Wing weighs 925 pounds wet, Harley's Electra Glide Ultra Classic weighs 890 pounds wet, and Kawasaki's Vulcan 2000 Classic weights 884 pounds wet. If you aren't an experienced rider, keeping these big bikes under control will require so much work on your part that you'll never develop proper riding skills. Once you've been riding awhile, a touring bike will likely be the most practical motorcycle you can buy; but earn your chops as a rider and develop good riding skills before jumping into one.

Just because your ride isn't classified as a touring bike doesn't mean you can't travel distances on your motorcycle. Any bike can be used for touring. In fact, when set up with windshields, saddlebags, and comfortable saddles, middleweight cruisers make great touring bikes. You won't be able to bring everything you own with you on a trip with your middleweight cruiser, but most people bring far too much junk with them when they travel, anyway (having lots of luggage capacity on a bike just encourages people to bring too much stuff). You should be able to get everything you need for any trip, no matter how long, into a couple of saddlebags and maybe a tank bag and a tailpack.

Sport-Tourers

Another category of touring bike is the sport-tourer. Like the cruiser category, this one is a little tough to define. Sometimes things get grouped together not because they are anything in particular, but because they are something that others are not. That's about as good a description of a sport-tourer as you'll find.

This type of bike can range from enormous machines like Honda's ST1300, which weighs 730 pounds wet, to a small motorcycle like the MZ Skorpion Traveller, a German bike built in the 1990s and early 2000s that is claimed to weigh in at 416 pounds dry. The only common characteristic among sport-tourers is usually just a set of hard saddlebags; other than that, they can come in just about any size and engine configuration imaginable.

The basic idea behind a sport-touring bike is that it combines the handling and performance of a sport bike with the comfort and convenience of a touring bike. BMW created the mold for this type of motorcycle. Until the late 1990s when it got into the business of building heavyweight touring bikes, just about every motorcycle the German company ever built could be considered a sport-touring bike. Even the company's GS-series bikes, which were classified as dual sports, were really more sport-touring type motorcycles.

Harley-Davidson was one of the first companies besides BMW to build a motorcycle that fit the German sport-touring mold. In 1983 Harley introduced the FXRT. In a lot of ways, this was an advanced motorcycle, at least for Harley. It had a rubber-mounted engine, five-speed transmission, sporty wind-tunnel-designed fairing, and a decent pair of hard saddlebags. Unfortunately it still had the old cast-iron Shovelhead engine. Most of the bugs had been worked out of the Shovelhead by that time, but it still used technology that the rest of the world had abandoned twenty years earlier.

In 1984 the FXRT used an Evolution motor—no more Shovelhead. When I saw my first Evo-powered FXRT, I got rid of the Shovelhead I was riding at the time and bought the FXRT. It might not have been the best motorcycle made, but at the time I considered it the best Harley. I rode FXRTs until 2000, when I switched to Road Kings.

Later in the 1980s Kawasaki introduced the first real Japanese sport-tourer, the Concours, and not long after Honda introduced its idea of a sport-tourer, the ST1100. These were good motorcycles; if they had been built by an American company, I might have bought one myself. I remember when I saw my first ST1100 in the early 1990s. I loved the look of that sleek, black machine. (I still love the look of the current 1300-cc version.)

Then other European companies like Triumph, Ducati, Moto Guzzi, and Aprilia started building sport-tourers. Today pretty much every motorcycle company still in business builds some kind of sport-tourer. Some might even argue that my Vision is a sport-tourer, though it's a little too big to qualify in my opinion. Even many of the bikes that are small enough to qualify as sport-tourers are too big for a newer rider to manage. They tend to be tall, with a lot of bodywork and luggage carried up high. This increases cornering clearance, allowing them to lean way over in fast corners, but it also makes them top-heavy and thus clumsy to manage at slower speeds. Cruisers carry their weight lower to the ground, making them feel less like they are about to tip over at low speeds. Because of this, a cruiser that weighs more than a sport-tourer can actually feel lighter.

Another disadvantage of sport-tourers, at least for newer riders, is that they are covered with expensive bodywork that can break if the bike tips over. The sad fact is that when you are learning to ride, you will most likely have a minor tip over or two. I can't remember my first tip over, but I've had a few. I'd like to say I haven't tipped my current bike, but shit happens. Even though my Vision has a lot of bodywork, it's well designed, with stop plates underneath that are the only parts that come into contact with the ground and hold the bike at a forty-five-degree angle in the event of a low-speed tip over. Most bikes with plastic bodywork hit the ground plastic first, which can get expensive. It seems the designers at Victory understand that motorcycles inevitably fall over. If you ride long enough, you will fall down; hopefully it will only happen when you are going slowly.

Even with all the plastic bodywork, a midsized sport-tourer can make a good choice for a newer rider, especially a newer rider who's fairly tall—just make sure you carry good insurance. If that's the type of bike you like, you'll find that most midsized sport-tourers are practical, comfortable, and versatile motorcycles.

Sport Bikes

Back in the 1950s and 1960s Americans weren't the only people modifying their motorcycles; Europeans were doing the same thing, only they had a different aim in mind when they started customizing their bikes. Compared with America's long stretches of straight, wide-open highways, Europe is much more condensed, with narrow, twisting streets, crowded high-speed freeways, and winding mountain passes. Americans need bikes that are stable in a crosswind on an open road, so we tend to go for motorcycles that are long and low; Europeans have to dodge fast-moving traffic on streets that often are older than the oldest American city.

The different needs of American riders and European riders go back so far that you can see them reflected in the types of saddles used on horses. American-style saddles put the rider in a roomy, stretched-out, upright position; European-style saddles had the rider leaning forward in a racer-type crouch, his or her legs tucked up behind.

When the Europeans, particularly the Brits, started modifying their motorcycles, instead of building long, low, stretched-out choppers, they copied European horse riding: low-mounted handlebars, footpegs set high and back, and cut-down saddles. This put the rider into a forward-leaning racer-type riding position. The Brits called this kind of custom a "café racer," because their riders often raced from one café to another.

This style of motorcycle was slow to catch on in the United States. Throughout the 1960s and 1970s most European and Japanese manufacturers equipped bikes sold in Europe with low handlebars and rearset footpegs, whereas bikes shipped to the U.S. market featured lower, forward-mounted footpegs and higher handlebars, which were often called "western-style" bars, because they had a sort of cowboylike look to them.

BMW brought the R90S, a café racer with a small fairing—more of a headlight shroud, since it didn't do much to protect the rider from the elements—to the U.S. market in 1973. Harley followed suit with the XLCR Sportster ("XL" is Harley's designation for the Sportster engine, and "CR" stood for "café racer") in 1977, but its model wasn't very successful and was the last sport-type motorcycle to wear the Harley brand until the recently introduced XR1200. Other than an oddball European bike imported into the country in extremely small quantities, café racers were thinly represented in the United States in the 1970s.

That was about to change, thanks in large part to the development of superbike racing. By the mid-1970s road-racing motorcycles had become so specialized that they literally no longer shared a single part with their road-going counterparts. At that time most road bikes were powered by large-displacement four-stroke engines while road-racing bikes were powered almost exclusively by purpose-built two-stroke mid-displacement engines.

Historically motorcycle racing had been something that an average motorcyclist could do. Back in the early days most clubs formed around racing; early clubs like the Boozefighters focused as much on racing as they did on raising hell. Remember, this was a time when you'd ride one motorcycle to work every day, then race that same bike on the weekend. But by the 1970s a person who wanted to race competitively had to buy a purpose-built race bike that cost half a year's salary, if you had a good job. Racing had changed from something that anyone with a motorcycle could do into an elite activity.

At just about the time that two strokes completely took over the top levels of racing, an alternative form of racing based on production bikes started to gain popularity. This happened when the Japanese introduced their big, powerful four-cylinder machines. Magazines called these "superbikes," so the production class in which these motorcycles raced became known as the "superbike" class.

Production-based classes reinvigorated the sport of motorcycle racing at a grassroots level. In the early days of superbike racing, anyone with $2,500 could walk into one of the thousands of Kawasaki or Suzuki shops that could be found in any small town and buy a production bike capable of being built into a competitive racer. Within a few years thousands of people were competing in club races all across the United States. Due to the popularity of this type of racing, manufacturers began offering sportier and sportier motorcycles. Racers liked these bikes because it was less work (and less expense) to convert them into race bikes, but a lot of nonracers bought them, too, just because they liked the style of the bikes.

At first these bikes differed little from the standard bikes of the day. They had lower handlebars, maybe a small café-racer fairing, or at least a set of footpegs moved back a few inches from the standard position. But as superbike racing grew in popularity, the manufacturers got into the sport with factory-supported teams, which meant they started making production bikes with specifications that approached those of full-on race bikes. This is how we got the first factory crotch rockets, the Honda Interceptors, Kawasaki Ninjas, Yamaha FZRs, and Suzuki GSX-Rs.

These bikes became more and more capable, until they reached a point where it was virtually impossible (and completely insane) for riders to come anywhere near reaching their limits on public roads. Today's crotch rockets are more potent than the pure racing bikes of a generation ago.

High-performance sport bikes are poor choices for beginners. Any of the 600-cc class sport bikes qualifies as one of the highest-performance machines you can buy of any type; probably only Formula 1 race cars generate more power per cubic inch than the engines in 600-cc sport bikes. But as mentioned in the last chapter, sport bikes don't generate much torque. Because of this they are difficult for a newer rider to ride smoothly in traffic.

In fact, I don't recommend anyone use modern sport bikes for daily transportation on public roads. I dislike telling people what they should and shouldn't ride, and if you want to ride a crotch rocket, you have the freedom to do so—sport bikes are popular and a lot of people use them for everyday transportation without any problems. But that said, I believe this type of motorcycle is best left to the racetrack. It's great fun to get out on a track and put your knees down on the pavement in high-speed corners, but out on the street that type of riding will just get you killed, and probably sooner rather than later. And when you're riding on this type of bike, you'll be tempted to ride it like you stole it every time you throw your leg over the saddle.

Even if you have the self-restraint needed to keep from exploring your motorcycle's limits on public roads, sport bikes are excruciatingly uncomfortable to ride. The racer crouch is ideal when you're on a track, throwing yourself from side to side, putting your knee down in the corners, and accelerating hard in the straights, but for the rest of the time, riding laid out over the gas tank puts a lot of strain on your body.

Sport bikes are especially bad in stop-and-go traffic, where you have to crane your neck back so far to see what's going on around you that your head is likely to stick in that position. Unless you're extremely young (and I mean young, like so young your fontanel has barely hardened over), if you put serious miles on a sport bike, you'd better keep a chiropractor on your payroll.

Standards
In 1980 most of the motorcycles you could buy were still basic do-it-all type machines, much like the BSA

Gold Star had been thirty years earlier. Most companies built a basic type of motorcycle and only modified it slightly for different uses. To make a cruiser, a company would take its basic bike, add a pull-back handlebar and a stepped saddle (the magazines called them "buckhorn" bars and "king-queen" saddles back then), and give it a coat of black paint. The same bike might get a square headlight and a square plastic rear fender cover, maybe a fork brace or an oil cooler, and that would be sold as the sport-bike version.

The only companies making touring bikes at that time were Harley-Davidson and BMW. The Japanese manufacturers began to offer touring and racing accessories, but these amounted to tinkering around at the margins; the basic motorcycle underneath remained more or less the same. But everything changed during the 1980s. Cruisers evolved into carbon copies of Harley-Davidson motorcycles, complete with V-twin engines; touring bikes sprouted barn-door-sized fairing and enough luggage capacity to carry the entire belongings of a small third-world village; and sport bikes developed full racing fairings, complete with uncomfortable racer positions. At the beginning of the decade you could count the number of bikes made with any sort of fairing on one hand; by the end of the decade the only bikes that didn't have plastic fairings were the Harley-style cruisers.

As the 1990s rolled around, it seemed like no one was building an ordinary, all-around motorcycle anymore. The manufacturers noticed this and introduced what the motorcycle press called a "new" type of motorcycle: the standard. In reality, this was just the rebirth of the regular old all-around motorcycle.

Like "sport-tourer," "standard" is a bit of a garbage category. The only thing that most standards have in common is the lack of a fairing and luggage. Standards range from tiny beginner bikes like the Suzuki TU250 to BMW's wild K1300R, which is a type of standard often called a "street fighter" (street fighters are standards in that they have no bodywork but have the guts of high-performance sport bikes).

Though some of the high-performance street fighters might be a handful for newer riders to control, generally speaking, standards make good choices for first bikes. They tend to have comfortable riding positions and tractable engines, and like most cruisers, they don't have expensive bodywork to break when you inevitably drop your bike.

WHAT YOU SHOULD KNOW

- Don't worry about what everyone else thinks; pick the bike you like.
- Custom choppers and antique bikes might look cool, but they aren't practical to use as transportation.
- The less bodywork you have on a bike, the less it costs if you tip over, which is an important consideration for newer riders.

CHAPTER THREE

THE FUNDAMENTALS OF RIDING

ou may think the next logical step would be to buy a bike. After all, how can you learn to ride if you don't have a bike? For most of the time I've been riding, the answer was that you couldn't learn to ride unless you had a bike, but over the past twenty or so years that's changed, thanks to the Motorcycle Safety Foundation. Originally formed in 1973, the MSF started out as a trade organization that promoted motorcycle manufacturers as much as it furthered safety. In some ways it still is that; its current sponsors are BMW, Ducati, Harley-Davidson, Honda, Kawasaki, KTM, Piaggio/Vespa, Suzuki, Triumph, Victory, and Yamaha, and ultimately the MSF serves those companies.

But early on the major bike companies figured

out that one of the best ways the MSF could serve them was by helping to keep as many of their customers alive as possible. You'd be hard-pressed to find an organization that has done more to promote motorcycle safety than the MSF, not just in the past thirty-some years since it was founded, but ever. Back in the early years of the MSF, motorcycle fatalities were on the rise, and they had been for the previous decade. In 1980 motorcycle-related fatalities in the United States peaked at 5,144 deaths. That same year the MSF sponsored the first International Motorcycle Safety Conference. This marked the beginning of serious research into the causes of motorcycle-related deaths. The following year the government published *Motorcycle Accident Cause Factors and Identification of Countermeasures,* which is usually referred to as the "Hurt Report," in honor of its primary author Harry Hurt.

Among its findings, the Hurt Report noted that 92 percent of riders involved in accidents lacked any formal motorcycle training; they were either self-taught, or they'd learned from family and friends. Apparently the riders' friends had passed on their own bad habits, because the report noted: "Motorcycle riders in these accidents showed significant collision avoidance problems. Most riders would overbrake and skid their rear wheel, and underbrake the front wheel, greatly reducing collision avoidance deceleration. The ability to countersteer and swerve was essentially absent."

Clearly someone needed to develop a formal motorcycle training course, but there was no obvious organization to handle that job. You might think the government would step in, but it seems that motorcycle riders are a low priority for most elected officials. The Hurt Report did nothing to light a fire under the government's collective ass to start developing and funding rider training programs.

Thankfully, the MSF stepped up and did what all levels of government were unable to do: develop a rider training program. The MSF's RiderCourse made its debut in California in 1987. Within a few years it had spread across the country. Not only do all states offer MSF RiderCourses, but the majority of them use some form of the RiderCourse curriculum in their licensing tests. Many states allow completion of the course itself to fulfill the riding skills portion of the licensing exam—complete the RiderCourse, get your motorcycle endorsement.

One of the best aspects of the RiderCourse is that in most states the program provides the motorcycles you'll use to complete the course (and often earn your motorcycle license). That means that you can learn to ride without even buying a bike, which is why I put this chapter on learning to ride before the chapter on buying a motorcycle. Many of the programs that offer the courses even provide protective gear, which will save you hundreds or even thousands of dollars. Taking a RiderCourse is the best way to find out if you even like riding a motorcycle before you spend a small fortune buying a bike and all the associated gear.

I'm going to provide you with the basics of motorcycle riding in the following pages, but first I'm going to give you the single most important piece of advice in this entire book—***complete the MSF RiderCourse.***

And if you're already an experienced motorcyclist who hasn't taken the basic RiderCourse, take one of the advanced training courses. If you're self-taught, or if you learned to ride from a friend or family member, chances are you've developed some bad habits over the years. Riding is an extremely high-risk activity and even if those bad habits haven't caused you problems so far, sooner or later your luck will run out. It's best to rely on luck as little as possible; one of the best ways to do that is to get formal training. It's the most important thing you can do to avoid getting maimed or killed. I advise you to use what I write here to help familiarize yourself with the operation of a motorcycle to help you pass the MSF RiderCourse.

THE SIX BASIC CONTROLS

Operating a motorcycle is a complex activity. You'll need to use both of your hands and both of your feet to operate the controls, and you'll often be using all of them at the same time. Remember, you'll also need to use your feet to hold yourself up when the bike is stopped. Believe it or not, I've seen people forget this and fall over at a stop.

You'll have to master six basic controls to ride most motorcycles. For the first twenty or so years I rode motorcycles, manufacturers used different layouts for these main controls. I only rode Harleys, but even though all the bikes I rode were built by the same manufacturer, the location of the brakes, shifters, and clutches varied from model to model and from year to year. Having to relearn the controls each time you bought a new bike annoyed the hell out of us, and it could even be dangerous at times, but for the 1975 model year the U.S. government passed a law standardizing the location of many of those controls. Since the U.S. motorcycle market was the most important one for most manufacturers, virtually all of them adopted the layout specified by U.S. law.

The main controls on a motorcycle are as follows:

- **Throttle:** On a motorcycle the throttle is a twist grip that controls your speed, located on the right end of the handlebar.
- **Front brake lever:** This is a lever that controls the front brake, mounted on the right side of the handlebar, in front of the throttle.
- **Rear brake lever:** This is a lever that operates the rear brake, located near the right footpeg.
- **Clutch lever:** This is a lever that operates the clutch, located on the left side of the handlebar, in front of the left handgrip.
- **Shift lever:** This is a lever that shifts gears in the transmission, located near the left footpeg.
- **Handlebar:** Anyone who's ridden a bicycle knows what this is.

SECONDARY CONTROLS

IN ADDITION TO THESE six primary controls, you'll have to operate a variety of secondary controls when you're riding on public roads. The locations of these

aren't as standardized as are the locations for the primary controls, but the vast majority of motorcycle
manufacturers use the same basic layout. Secondary
controls include the following:

- **Ignition switch.** This can be found in all sorts
  of odd places, from up by the instruments, to
  the top of the tank, to below the seat. This operates much like the switch in a car, except that it
  doesn't actually start the bike, as it does in most
  cars. For that you'll need to use . . .

- **The electric start button.** This button, which
  engages the electric starting motor, is usually
  found on the right handgrip.

- **The choke or enrichment circuit.** This is a
  lever, usually on the left handgrip, that engages
  a choke on carbureted bikes or an enrichment or
  fast-idle circuit on fuel-injected bikes. Up until
  just a few years ago all bikes had these, but as
  motorcycle fuel-injection technology advances,
  more and more bikes skip this control.

- **Engine kill switch.** This is an emergency shut-
  off switch for the engine. I rarely if ever find the
  need to use this.

- **Turn signals.** Like cars, all modern street bikes
  have turn signals. The location and method
  of operation used for these varies a bit among
  some manufacturers—particularly Harley-
  Davidson and BMW—but on most bikes the
  control consists of a switch on the left handgrip
  that you push left to engage the left turn signal,
  push right to engage the right turn signal, and
  push straight in to turn off the signals. Unlike

all modern cars, many bikes don't have self-canceling turn signals, so you'll need to remember to shut these off or you'll be riding down the road with your signal flashing. In addition to being embarrassing, this can be dangerous.

- **Horn.** This is a button located on one of the handgrips—usually the left—that activates your motorcycle's horn. Many people are afraid to use their horns because they think it's rude, but it's not nearly as rude as getting mangled by a car. If other drivers don't see you, don't worry about being rude; use your horn to let them know you're there. It could save your life.

- **Headlight dimmer switch.** This works the same as the dimmer switch in your car. I don't use this much because I always leave my headlight on high beam during the day, when I do most of my riding.

- **Speedometer.** This indicates your speed, just as it does in your car. Unlike cars, which usually feature analog speedometers, a lot of motorcycles use digital speedometers.

- **Tachometer.** This indicates your engine rpm, again just as it does in your car. Because almost all motorcycles use manual transmissions, these are much more useful on motorcycles than they are in cars, which mostly use automatic transmissions.

PRERIDE INSPECTION

MOTORCYCLES HAVE COME A long way since I started riding, but they still require more care and maintenance than cars. Even if a motorcycle was as reliable as a car, you'd still want to be extra diligent about making sure everything was in working order because the consequences of a system failing are much more extreme on a bike.

The MSF Experienced RiderCourse, which I have taken, teaches the following preride inspection technique, called "T-CLOCK":

- T: Tires and wheels
- C: Controls
- L: Lights and electrics
- O: Oil and fluids
- C: Chassis and chain
- K: Kickstand

I'll be honest; I check these items fairly regularly, but I don't check each one every time I ride. Some items I do check, if not daily, almost every day. If I rode a bike with a chain, I'd check that every day, but I don't: my bike uses a belt, which requires very little maintenance. I also check my tires and wheels every time I ride. I look them over to make certain they're not damaged or low on air. I'll visually inspect them to make sure they haven't picked up any nails or glass, but I only check the air pressure once every two or three days unless I suspect one of them might have a leak.

Similarly I don't check my oil level every day, at least on my Vision, which doesn't burn a lot of oil. If I'm riding a Harley that I know burns some oil, I'll check it often, sometimes more than once a day if I put on a lot of miles.

I'll check my lights fairly regularly to make certain they're working, especially my taillight and brake light, which I can't see while I'm riding. The consequences of a malfunctioning taillight or brake light may be getting rear-ended by a car, and as you might imagine, that falls under the category of "really bad." It seems like every car driver who has hit a motorcycle has said "I didn't see the motorcycle." Most of the time the real story is that the driver wasn't paying attention, but in my opinion, if your taillight or brake light isn't working, you're as much at fault as the driver who just hit you.

I'm always paying attention to how my controls are working, but I can't say I check these things every time I ride. Controls and cables on modern bikes are far more reliable than they were back when the MSF devised the T-CLOCK method. I do check for loose bolts in the chassis every now and then, but that was a bigger issue when I rode Harley-Davidson motorcycles, which vibrate much more than my Victory does. If you ride a Harley, you'll probably want to check the bolts and nuts on a daily basis.

CHECKING TIRES

THE ONE THING I do consider critical to check frequently is the air pressure in my tires. I've had tires go flat while I was flying down the road. I don't want it to happen again if there's anything I can do to help it. Besides, a motorcycle handles best when the tires are inflated to the proper pressure. Riding with the proper air pressure in your tires also ensures that your tires will last longer. This can save you a lot of money over time.

You'll need to consult your owner's manual to find out the proper pressure for your tires. On the sidewall of your tire you'll find text saying something like: "Maximum Air Pressure 43 PSI." That means that 43 pounds is the maximum air pressure your tire can safely handle, but that doesn't mean that your bike was designed to operate with tires pumped up to 43 PSI. More likely your bike was designed to run in the 34–38 PSI range, and inflating your tires beyond that point will adversely affect handling and also cause your tires to wear out faster.

I always keep a tire pressure gauge in my motorcycle tool kit. I've found that it's difficult to get a gauge on the valve stems on some motorcycles with a lot of luggage and bodywork. The area in which you will be working can be tight, and a long gauge can be difficult to seat properly on the valve stem. I carry a small round gauge with a dial instead of a long one with a stick that pokes out to indicate the air pressure; I find the smaller gauge is easier to maneuver around the tire and wheel.

When you check the air pressure, you should take a few seconds to make sure all the axle bolts and pinch bolts on the fork and shocks are tight. I once was riding with a buddy when the bolts securing the clamps that held his front axle in place came loose. His front wheel fell off and his bike went end over end in the ditch. Amazingly, he seemed all right after the incident, and so we continued on our way to the rally we were attending. But to this day he remembers nothing of that weekend.

COUNTERSTEERING

YOU NEED TO UNDERSTAND countersteering before you think about starting up your motorcycle. If you've never ridden a motorcycle, you're going to find it's unlike any other vehicle you've ever ridden or driven. You control a motorcycle by leaning into corners rather than turning into them. The closest thing to riding a motorcycle is probably flying an airplane. Like a plane, a motorcycle rotates on a central axis. Imagine a line running through the center of the motorcycle-rider combination. This is the central axis.

To initiate a turn, you countersteer the bike. No subject in motorcycling generates more debate than countersteering, and most of the people doing the arguing don't really understand the principle. Even though they don't understand it, they use it every time they ride. Most of them just don't realize they're doing it.

You countersteer a motorcycle every time you ride at any speed faster than a slow jog. It's the quickest and most efficient way to lean a motorcycle into a turn. It's pretty simple when you get down to the mechanics of it: you press the handlebar on the side in which you want to turn. If you are turning left, press the left handgrip. If you want to go right, press the right handgrip.

This may seem backward, and it would be on a different type of vehicle, like an ATV or a snowmobile. If you press the left handgrip of an ATV it would turn the front wheels to the right, thus causing the ATV to turn right. The same thing happens when you press on the left handgrip of a motorcycle;

this also makes the front wheel move slightly to the right. But unlike a four-wheeled vehicle like an ATV, when the front wheel of a motorcycle moves to the right at any rate above a fast-walking speed, it leans the motorcycle to the left and initiates a turn to the left. Once the motorcycle is leaned over at the correct angle to complete the turn, you release enough pressure for the front tire to fall to the left and the bike goes to the left.

In other words, once you've initiated the lean with countersteering, you steer through a corner as you would any other vehicle—countersteering only gets you leaned into the turn in the first place. The thing is, the turning you do after you're leaned over is so slight that you won't even notice it; you just notice the countersteering pressure needed to initiate the lean in the first place. In fact, you'll probably feel like you're countersteering all the way through the corner.

In some instances you will continue to use countersteering in a corner. If the corner tightens up—if it's what is called a "decreasing radius" corner—you may need to use countersteering to lean the bike over farther so that you turn sharper. This is where understanding countersteering will save your life. If a corner surprises you and gets tighter midcorner, you have two choices: turn sharper and make it through the corner, or run wide and either ride off the road and have a terrible crash or ride into oncoming traffic and initiate a head-on collision, depending on which direction you're going. If you can't sharpen up your turn by countersteering and leaning the motorcycle farther over, the first option won't be available to you.

Larger bikes require more pressure to make the

bike bend into its initial lean. You may feel like you need to pull on the opposite handgrip as well as push on the original handgrip. That's because the larger a bike is, the more pressure it will require to initiate countersteering. This is a good reason to start out with a smaller motorcycle.

CRANKING IT OVER

WHEN YOU FIRST RIDE your new motorcycle, make sure you do so in a safe place where there's not any traffic. I recommend finding an empty parking lot. Even if you have your license, it's still a good idea to familiarize yourself with your new machine in a place where you don't have to worry about other people hurting you so you can concentrate on not hurting yourself.

If your bike has a center stand, place it up on that. A lot of Japanese and European bikes have center stands; unfortunately most American bikes don't have them. I think this is one area where the other countries have us beat, because a center stand is one of the handiest features a bike can have. They make most maintenance jobs a lot easier, and they're much less prone to sinking into the tarmac on hot days.

Center stands are easy to use, provided you use them the right way. The trick is to follow the proper procedure:

1. First, stand beside the bike, facing it from the left side, and grasp both handlebar grips.

2. When you have a firm grip on the bike, take your right foot and lower the center stand until you feel both its feet resting securely on the ground.

3. While keeping downward pressure on the center stand with your foot, balance the bike by the handlebars so that it rests perfectly upright.

4. There will most likely be some kind of handle down below the rear part of the saddle (some newer bikes will have a retractable handle); grasp the handle. If there's no handle, grab the frame below the saddle.

5. Lock the center stand tang (the metal tab sticking up from the bottom of the center stand) in place with the heel of your boot so that it doesn't slide around. Make certain you have a good bite on it with your boot.

6. Push downward and rearward with your boot while rolling the bike backward with your arms.

As long as you're using your leg to do the actual lifting and just using your upper body to roll the bike backward, the bike should roll right up on the center stand. If you're not lifting with your leg but rather lifting with your arms, you probably won't be able to get the bike up on the center stand. It's easy if you do it right; it's impossible if you do it wrong. It doesn't even matter how big the bike is. If you do it right, it's almost as easy to lift an 1800-cc Gold Wing as it is to lift a 250-cc Rebel. If you do it wrong, you'll have your hands full with the Rebel, and you can forget about the Gold Wing.

If your bike lacks a center stand, straddle the bike (remember, you always get on a motorcycle from the left side because the kickstand is on the left, so it will be leaning that way), hold both handgrips securely, and squeeze both the clutch and the front brake lever. You'll need to hold the clutch lever in to start most motorcycles, and holding the front brake lever in will keep the motorcycle from rolling when you start it.

If you don't have a center stand, you'll have to climb aboard the bike and hold it up yourself. When you're standing securely over the bike with one leg on each side, raise the bike up so that it stands upright. Once you've comfortably balanced the bike, you can rest your weight on the seat. Remember to raise the kickstand up, since many bikes won't run with the kickstand down. Even if a bike doesn't have a circuit that kills the engine if the kickstand is down, you still want to make sure you raise it up because if you ride off with it down it could catch on something and cause you to crash.

Next, turn your ignition key to "on" and make sure the kill switch is not in the "off" position. I've seen more than one person wear out a battery trying to start a bike while the kill switch was in the "off" position.

With your left foot, make sure the bike is in neutral. You will see a green light on the dash that indicates the bike is in neutral, but a word of warning—don't always trust that light. I've ridden many bikes that have a neutral light that will come on when the transmission isn't completely out of gear. I trust my left foot more than I trust my neutral light. I make sure that I can feel the bike is in neutral before

I start it. If you haven't yet developed a good feel for the shifter, release the clutch and brake levers and carefully roll the bike back and forth to see if the rear wheel spins freely. If it does, the bike is in neutral. (Don't forget to squeeze the clutch and front-brake levers again once you've gotten the bike into neutral.)

Once you've determined the bike is in neutral, turn on the choke or fast-idle circuit if your bike is so equipped, especially if the engine is cold. If it's been warmed up, you shouldn't have to bother with this. On a properly tuned modern motorcycle, you should now be able to push the starter button and start the motorcycle with no drama.

If the motorcycle doesn't start immediately, don't hold the starter button down. This will wear down the battery and can flood the engine or even burn out the starter motor. Instead, check for obvious problems. If there is a problem with your electrical system, you'll probably be able to hear the starter motor turning over sluggishly. If your bike is in good running condition with a good charging system, chances are that the problem is something as simple as your having bumped the kill switch into the "off" position. This is very easy to do.

Another possibility is that you may have a bike that needs just a bit of throttle to start properly. This indicates that something is not quite right in your carburetion or fuel-injection system, but the problem might be so minor that you'll never be able to track it down. Usually it's best to just figure out how much throttle you have to give your bike to start it.

This will be tricky, because the bike will likely

just require the slightest pressure on the throttle return spring; anything more than that will flood the engine with gas so that you won't be able to start the bike at all. Developing a feel for dealing with your throttle on start-up is an art, one you'll only be able to perfect with time and practice.

I've actually seen this procedure turned into art—I saw a professional comedian in Reno do a hilarious routine in which he reenacted the process of starting a carbureted Harley-Davidson. The bit lasted half an hour and was one of the funniest things I've ever seen. Fortunately for you, this is a novelty act that isn't performed very often out in the real world, thanks to modern motorcycle technology. As fuel-injection systems get better, this sort of problem is becoming increasingly rare.

ENGAGING THE CLUTCH

CHANGING GEARS WHILE RIDING a motorcycle is similar to driving a car with a manual transmission, except that you use your hands on a bike to do what your feet do in a car, and you use your feet on a bike to do what your hands would do in a car. The clutch works the same in a bike as it does in a car: it disengages the transmission from the engine. You just operate the lever with your hand instead of your foot. When you have the clutch lever pulled in all the way to the handgrip, the transmission is disengaged. As you let the clutch out, the plates in the clutch come into contact with each other and connect the transmission to the crankshaft.

The area in the travel of the clutch lever where the plates start to come into contact with each other is what the MSF calls the "friction zone." As the plates engage, the motorcycle starts to move forward. To find the friction zone, pull the clutch lever toward the handgrip and shift the transmission into first gear. To do this, push the lever down with your foot. Then, with both feet planted firmly on the ground, keep holding down the front brake lever and slowly let out the clutch lever. When the bike starts to move forward, you're in the friction zone. As soon as the bike starts to roll, pull the clutch back in and stop. If you don't, you'll kill the engine because you're still holding the front brake lever. Do this a couple of times to get a feel for where the friction zone begins.

HITTING THE BRAKES

You're just about ready to start your parking lot practice, but before you start riding, you need to make sure you can stop. Stopping will require you to use both of your hands and both of your feet, all at the same time. In one motion you'll pull in the clutch lever with your left hand, let off the throttle, squeeze the front brake lever with your right hand, push down on the rear brake lever with your right foot, and downshift with your left foot. And when it's all over, you'll have to remember to put down your feet to hold up the bike. Again, it's not that different from stopping a car, except that you have one more brake control to deal with and you'll need to hold up the bike once you've stopped.

It's critically important that you use your front brake when stopping. An average motorcycle relies on its front brakes for 70 to 80 percent of its stopping power. Bikes with a more rearward weight distribution, like long cruisers, rely a bit more on their rear brakes, but the front is still the most important. Short wheelbase sport bikes barely rely on their rear brakes at all. In fact, if you watch a motorcycle race, you'll see that the rear wheels of most of the bikes are slightly off the ground as they brake hard for a turn. On a racetrack, you mostly use your rear brake to settle the chassis in a corner; you use it very little, if at all, for stopping duty.

You'll want to develop a good feel for your brakes because good brake control will save your life more than any other skill. The Hurt Report mentioned earlier in this chapter found that not using the front brake and locking up the rear brake was a factor in the majority of fatalities, and recent reports by various state agencies have found that this is still the case.

Motorcycle manufacturers have recognized how deadly this problem is, and some high-end motorcycles now use linked braking systems with valves that direct a percentage of the braking force from the rear brake pedal to the front wheel. This makes it much easier to engage in quick, straight emergency stops, but the technology is generally used only on the most expensive motorcycles, like my Victory Vision, and Honda's Gold Wing. Most likely you'll have to develop your braking skills on a bike that isn't equipped with this technology.

If you lock up the brakes and go into a skid, it will be something of a miracle if you don't crash. If you're lucky, you'll just fall down and slide down the road. If you're not lucky, you'll have a high-side type accident, as discussed earlier.

TAKING OFF

Now THAT YOU'VE GOT a handle on what you need to do to stop and where to find the friction zone of your clutch, you can finally start riding your motorcycle. To get moving, find the friction zone of your clutch once again, only this time you're going to release the clutch lever all the way and move through the friction zone. To do this you'll have to release the front brake, but remember to cover the brake lever with at least two fingers from your right hand so you can grab the brake and stop quickly in an emergency. Covering the brake is a good habit that you should have throughout your riding career.

As you ease out the clutch lever and get into the friction zone, twist the throttle to give the engine just enough gas to start moving smoothly. Too little throttle and you'll stall the engine; too much throttle and you'll spin out and crash or even wheelie over backward, which are both terrible ways to start out your first ride. If at any time you feel you are not in complete control of the bike, pull in the clutch and apply the brakes to stop.

Because almost every motorcycle has a manual transmission, you'll need to shift gears once you get rolling. It works just like in a car—when your engine reaches a certain rpm, you need to shift up a gear to avoid overrevving. When your engine drops below a certain rpm, you need to downshift to avoid stalling the engine. Your goal is to keep your engine in what's known as the "powerband," which is the rpm range in which an engine generates power most efficiently.

Overrevving can cause your engine to blow up in extreme cases, but underrevving an engine can do damage, too. It can lead to detonation, which is when there are tiny explosions inside the engine that can damage components, and it can also cause the buildup of unburned carbon deposits. But the main problem with letting the rpm level drop below the engine's powerband is that when this happens you won't have the ability to accelerate out of danger.

If your brakes are your primary tools for avoiding crashes, the ability to accelerate runs a close second. Sometimes it's better to accelerate out of the way of danger than it is to brake to avoid it. If your engine is running below its efficient powerband and is bogging down, when you twist your throttle, there will be a pause before the engine reacts. If you're trying to get out of the way of a speeding car and this happens, you're probably not going to live very long. It's best to just make sure that your engine is in its powerband at all times so you'll always have the option of accelerating should you need it.

To shift up, roll off the throttle at the same time you squeeze in the clutch lever. When the throttle is fully closed and the clutch disengaged, move the shift lever up with your left toe in a firm, smooth movement until the lever stops. If you hesitate, your shifter might get caught between gears so that when you release the clutch and twist the throttle, your transmission will be in what's called "false neutral" and your engine will just spin without moving you forward. This can be deadly if you are trying to get out of the way of something, or if some jackass is following you too closely on the highway.

To downshift, roll off the throttle and squeeze the clutch. Firmly press down on the shift lever, and then apply a small amount of throttle as you ease out the clutch lever. You do this to match your engine speed to the speed of your rear wheel. If your rear wheel is going faster than your engine is spinning, you'll get wheel hop, which can lead to a dangerous skid.

When coming to a stop, you might shift all the way down to neutral without releasing the clutch, but you'll want to do this gradually because you can damage your motorcycle's transmission by shifting down into too low a gear while you are moving, even with the clutch lever pulled in. This is especially true if your bike's clutch is starting to wear out.

This sounds a lot more complicated than it is. In recent years there's been a trend toward motorcycles with automatic transmissions, but I think this is happening because people think riding a manual-transmission bike will be too complicated. It really isn't. You'll quickly get the hang of it, and once you've got a few miles under your belt, shifting—and everything else associated with riding a motorcycle—will come as naturally to you as breathing.

GEARING UP

Before you do any of the preceding activities, you'll need to have proper riding gear. The minimum gear you should always wear when you ride includes the following:

- Helmet
- Riding jacket
- Full-finger gloves
- Long pants
- Over-the-ankle boots

Helmets

A lot of people are surprised when they find out I never ride without a helmet. Like most people my age, I did ride without a helmet for decades. We didn't even have helmets available to us when I started riding, so we never even gave them any thought. Then in 1983 I had throat cancer and had a laryngectomy. After that I didn't have a choice. The air passing over my laryngectomy made it impossible for me to breathe unless I wore a full-face helmet, so I either wore a helmet or I didn't ride. For me that was no choice at all—I started wearing a helmet and using a windshield.

Today I'd wear a helmet whether I needed to or not, and not just because they are safe; I find riding is more comfortable and enjoyable with a full-face helmet. It reduces road noise, keeps the wind blasts out of my face, and keeps bugs and other debris out of my eyes.

That said, there's no doubt that wearing a helmet is a lot safer than not wearing a helmet. Harry Hurt, of Hurt Report fame, conducted a long-term study of helmet use for the University of Southern California's Head Protection Research Laboratory and discovered that you are five times more likely to suffer a head injury if you crash without a helmet as you would be if you crashed while you were wearing one. Every study conducted since has backed up Hurt's findings.

This doesn't mean that a helmet is some sort of magic totem that will save you in every circumstance. If you get hit by a bus or crash into a guardrail at 80 miles per hour, you'll probably experience so much blunt trauma to your body that you won't survive even if you have a helmet. But for every extreme example like that there are many cases where a person without a helmet died from hitting his or her head in a minor tip over; had he or she been wearing a helmet, the person would have suffered only minor embarrassment.

Take Indian Larry, the custom bike builder from New York, for example. On Saturday, August 28, 2004, while filming an episode of *Biker Build-Off,* Larry was performing stunts for the crowd. He rode his stunt bike through a wall of flames and topped this off with his signature bike-surfing bit, standing up on the seat, his arms stretched out in a crucifix pose. But something went wrong. His bike was probably going too slow, no more than 30 miles per hour, and the front end began to wobble badly. Instead of leaning forward to grab the handlebars and then sitting back down in the saddle, as he might usually do, Larry fell backward off the bike and cracked his skull on the asphalt.

Everyone expected Larry to get back up. When he didn't, friends and the film crew ran to his side. No one could quite believe it was happening. Larry had performed that stunt thousands of times. He knew what he was doing. Had he been wearing a helmet, he would have just been embarrassed on camera, but he wasn't, and on Monday, August 30, Indian Larry died. The guy was a good rider with decades of experience. If it could happen to him, it could happen to any of us.

It doesn't matter to me if you wear a helmet for comfort or wear it for safety. It doesn't matter to me if you don't wear any helmet at all. It's a free country and what you do is your business, not mine. Just know that I think you should wear a full-face helmet. If you don't and crack your skull and kill yourself, don't expect me to feel sorry for you.

If you do the sensible thing and decide to wear a helmet, make sure you get one that is comfortable. If you're like me, you'll practically live in your helmet, so it's worthwhile to spend a little extra money to get one that fits and has good ventilation. The only way you'll know if a helmet fits will be to try it on.

Different helmets fit different-shaped heads. I find that Nolan helmets fit me the best. My coauthor, Darwin, is of Swedish and Norwegian descent. Some people call Swedes "round heads" and Norwegians "square heads." There might be some truth to both stereotypes because he has a hard time finding helmets to fit his misshapen head. He finds that Shoei helmets fit him the best. You'll have to try on a bunch of different helmets to see which brands fit your head shape the best.

As for ventilation, that's tougher to test when trying on helmets in a motorcycle shop. Generally speaking, the more expensive the helmet, the better ventilation it will have. A well-ventilated helmet will flow so much air around your head that when you're riding at anything above a walking speed your head will be cooler with the helmet than without it. Believe it or not, when the temperature hits 110 degrees here in Arizona, wearing a well-ventilated helmet keeps me cooler than I would be if I rode without a helmet. When it comes to quality helmets, you usually get what you pay for.

Riding Jackets and Pants

When I started riding motorcycles, bikers had one option for a riding jacket: black leather. This was fine if you wanted to be Marlon Brando, but for those of us who identified with Chino there weren't a lot of options. That's changed completely now. Today you can get anything from one-piece Gore-Tex riding suits to fully armored mesh pants and jackets. To list all the options and features would take a complete chapter. At the very least you'll want a jacket with built-in armor to protect you in case of a crash.

If you ride a lot, you'll probably need at least two motorcycle jackets—one for warm weather and one for cold weather. Traditional leather jackets still work well for cooler weather, and you can get ventilated leather jackets for riding in warm weather if you like the look of leather.

Otherwise you can buy one of the riding suits from a company like Aerostich. These are the suits you see a lot of serious long-distance riders wearing. They are usually made of water-resistant materials like Gore-Tex, and can either be one-piece overall-type suits or traditional two-piece pants and jackets. These are nice if you commute to work on your motorcycle because you can wear them over your street clothes. The newer mesh riding suits are pretty nice, too. Most have built-in body armor, so they provide at least minimal protection in a crash, and they provide the maximum cooling in hot weather.

The minimum you want for leg protection is a pair of jeans. If you are riding around in shorts, you are a fool. If you crash, even at a low speed, you're going to spend years getting painful skin grafts. Plus you'll look like an idiot. Regular jeans are the bare minimum you should consider for riding motorcycles. Better yet would be a pair of jeans made especially for riding motorcycles, with built-in armor in the knees. Best of all would be leather motorcycle-specific pants, or at least a pair of Gore-Tex or mesh motorcycle pants.

I'll be honest—I've never worn gear with built-in armor, but I've been lucky. My coauthor, Darwin, hasn't been so fortunate—he took a low-speed spill a couple of years ago when he wasn't wearing armor and crushed his knee so severely that he'll walk with a limp for the rest of his life and will eventually need knee-replacement surgery. Armored jeans or riding pants may well have prevented much of the damage.

Boots and Gloves

Always wear a sturdy pair of gloves when riding motorcycles. Ideally you'll want a pair with gauntlets that extend over your wrists because these will prevent bees and other insects and debris from flying up your jacket sleeves while riding down the road. Having an angry hornet stinging your armpit can be a little distracting when you are riding through traffic. Motorcycle-specific gloves will have extra leather on the palms, fingers, and knuckles to provide extra protection in the event of a crash.

You'll also want to wear boots that go up over your ankles. If you see someone riding around in tennis shoes, or worse yet, sandals, you're probably seeing the same fool who wears shorts while riding. I recommend not getting too friendly with an idiot like that because then you'll have to go and visit him or her in the hospital while he or she is getting painful skin grafts.

Good boots serve a variety of purposes on a bike. First off, your feet are an important part of your motorcycle's suspension—after all, it's your legs that are suspending the bike when it's not moving. You want the contact points with the ground (your feet) to be as firm and secure as possible, so make sure your boots have grippy soles. If you go with cowboy boots, make sure they're work-type cowboy boots with rubber soles rather than the fashion-type boots with smooth leather soles, which are as slippery as banana peels. I wear cowboy boots and always make sure to get boots with rubber soles.

Your boots will also protect your feet, and not just in the event of a crash; every time you ride they'll protect your feet from getting burned by the exhaust pipes or getting hit by rocks thrown up by your front wheel.

What You Should Know

- Countersteering is the only way to get your bike to start turning at speeds faster than a walking pace.
- The front brake provides most of your stopping power; use it.
- Helmets not only protect your head, but they make riding more comfortable.

CHAPTER FOUR

EVALUATING A USED MOTORCYCLE

WHY BUY A USED MOTORCYCLE?

THE MOST COMPELLING REASON to buy a used motorcycle is to save money. Any new motorcycle you buy
will be worth much less money the moment you ride
it out of a dealership.

For many years Harley-Davidson motorcycles
were exceptions to this rule; when Harley built fewer
bikes than it could sell each year and their motorcycles were in short supply, you could buy a new bike
and turn around and sell it that same day for a profit.
But those days are long gone. Once you had to get
on a waiting list to buy a Harley, but now the Motor
Company builds more bikes than it can sell. As a

result, used Harleys are worth less than new ones. If you don't believe me, do a little snooping around the classifieds, Craigslist, or eBay and see what's selling.

In the old days when motorcycles wore out more quickly than they do today, you could make a good argument for not buying used bikes, but that no longer applies. Most motorcycles built today will outlast several owners. Unless you crash, it's pretty hard to wreck a modern motorcycle. Today's bikes will easily run for a hundred thousand or more miles, and most riders seldom put more than four thousand or five thousand miles per year on their bike. At that rate a modern bike should last for twenty or more years, so if you buy a five-year-old motorcycle that's in good shape, you should be set to ride for many years.

There are exceptions, though. Take Harley-Davidsons, again. While some Harleys might run forty thousand to fifty thousand miles without a rebuild, most of them are pretty tired by the time they hit the thirty-thousand-mile mark. When the Evolution engine came out in the 1980s, the California Highway Patrol ran their Harleys for thirty thousand miles, rebuilt the top ends of the engines, and then retired the bikes from active duty. They used them for training at the academy for a while before selling them, but they were no longer considered reliable enough for patrol work.

You can plan on rebuilding a Harley four or five times before a Honda wears out. I personally do not believe that any Harley will last longer than fifty to sixty thousand miles without a rebuild, regardless of how well maintained it is. Many Harley dealers won't accept a used Harley on trade if it has more than forty thousand miles on it, which tells me that their assessment of how long the bikes will run between engine rebuilds jibes with mine. On the other hand, at least you *can* rebuild your Harley; when your Honda wears out, it's done. Because of the way most Honda engines are constructed, it will probably cost you four times as much to rebuild a worn-out Honda as it will to buy another used Honda. This is why some people call Japanese motorcycles "disposable."

You'll also want to avoid motorcycles that have been raced or used heavily on racetracks. When I say a modern bike should be good for a hundred thousand or more miles, I'm talking about a hundred thousand street miles. A mile spent on a racetrack takes a lot more out of a bike than a mile spent on the street. If a bike has been raced or used for a lot of track days, all bets are off when it comes to reliability.

Fortunately there are ways to tell if a bike has been raced. If the bike has some sort of aftermarket bodywork on it, there's a good chance that it's been raced, or at least crashed heavily. Or it may have just been owned by some dipstick who fancied himself a racer, but the end result is the same.

A definitive way to see if a bike has been used on a racetrack is to check the axle bolts and the bolts holding on parts like brake calipers, footpegs, and shift and brake levers; if they have holes drilled in them, they've been safety wired. This is a sure sign that the bike has seen heavy track use. If you're buying a track bike to use on the track, then having a bike ready for safety wiring is a good thing, but for anyone buying a street bike for street use, evidence of safety wiring should be a big red flag that this bike has led an extremely hard life.

Although you can generally find good, reliable motorcycles in the used-bike market, the potential to get ripped off is high. The following information should help you negotiate the minefield that is the used-bike market.

A CAUTIONARY NOTE ABOUT RESURRECTING WRECKS

ONE OF THE CHEAPEST ways to buy a bike can be to find one that's been wrecked and rebuild it, but unless you're a seasoned motorcycle restorer, I recommend against this route. If you know what you are doing and enjoy that sort of work, then rebuilding a wrecked bike can be a rewarding process, but for most of us it's a complete pain in the ass.

Even if you have experience, chances are that the end result will be a bike that is never completely reliable. I used to ride with a guy who got all of his bikes this way, and even though he knew what he was doing, his bikes always suffered from niggling little problems.

Most of these resulted from the fact that the bike had sustained more structural damage in its crash than had been apparent when my buddy first examined it. An engine case might have a hairline crack, or a steering head might have been slightly tweaked, or some hidden piece of bent metal might have been wearing a hole in the wiring harness. My friend spent more time hunting down oil leaks and electrical gremlins than he did riding. I finally quit riding with the guy because I got sick of waiting for him while he made roadside repairs.

Trying to save money by rebuilding a wreck can also be an example of what the Brits call "false economy"; in the end you might spend more money trying to fix all the little problems than you would have spent buying a nonwrecked bike in the first place. Even if the damage to the bike is just cosmetic, you'll be shocked when you see how much bodywork and trim pieces for modern motorcycles cost. There are always exceptions to every rule, but generally speaking you'll probably save money by buying the best bike you can afford right from the start.

This brings up another potential hazard of buying used bikes—getting a bike with a salvage title. These are bikes that have been crashed and purchased from the owners by a salvage yard or an insurance company. This means that the motorcycle has been declared a total loss by a state's department of motor vehicles. "Total loss" means that the cost to fix the damage from a wreck would have exceeded the value of the motorcycle.

When a bike has been declared a total loss, any future owner who wants to license the bike has to create a new title for the vehicle, which will be marked as "salvage" by most states' motor vehicle departments. A few states allow the title to be resurrected as "clean" after some kind of inspection, but most states don't. Unless the title is cleaned in one of the few states that still allows this, the motorcycle will always be marked as a salvage-title vehicle.

Sometimes a motorcycle might end up with a salvage title because of superficial cosmetic damage, and the bike will be as good as new with a few new parts, but then again there's a good chance that the motorcycle might have suffered some serious structural damage when it was wrecked, structural damage that might not be readily apparent but will make itself known at the worst possible time, like when you're riding across Utah or Arizona on a 110-degree day.

Even if a bike didn't receive serious structural damage in a wreck, what are the odds that the same careless rider who crashed the motorcycle in the first place abused its engine or transmission to the point of failure before he or she wrecked the bike?

A related issue to watch out for is a bike with a salvage title that has been "cleaned" as just mentioned. Someone may have bought a wrecked bike, rebuilt it, and then exchanged the salvage title for a clean title in one of the states that still allows this sort of thing. The person then resells the bike as if it's never been wrecked, even though it is as likely to have serious problems as any other wrecked bike. Be wary of bikes that have been titled in several different states. This could be a sign that the bike has had its title cleaned, which in turn means that it's either been wrecked or, worse yet, stolen. In the latter case, you might have worse problems than an unreliable motorcycle; you might find yourself under arrest for receiving stolen property.

MECHANICAL INSPECTION

THE BEST WAY TO avoid buying a bike that's been wrecked is to have a professional mechanic examine the motorcycle before you buy it. This is a good idea for any used bike that you might buy, whether you buy it from a dealership or from a private seller.

If you know a motorcycle mechanic whom you trust, spend a few dollars to hire him or her to examine the bike. Otherwise do a little research to find a reputable shop where you can take the bike. If you're buying the bike from a shop, there's not much point in letting the shop staff examine the bike themselves, since they've already examined it. You're best off having a third-party mechanic who hasn't got a stake in selling the bike examine it. A shop or individual seller who won't let an outside mechanic examine a bike should be a bright red flag telling you to find a different bike.

To ensure the most objective mechanical inspection, take the bike to a shop that doesn't carry the brand of bike you're buying. Like all things, there are exceptions to this advice. For example, if you're buying a Ducati, which will have desmodromic valves (valves that are opened and closed mechanically, rather than being closed by valve springs, as on most engines), you probably won't learn much about the bike from your local Harley shop, where the mechanics are unfamiliar with overhead cams in general and probably wouldn't know a desmo valve from a pig's aorta. But in general you'll get the most unbiased opinion if you take a bike to a shop that doesn't sell that particular brand.

I understand that getting the bike professionally inspected will be a hassle and will cost you money, but the grief (and money) you might save yourself could make it worthwhile. It may even be impossible in some cases, but most dealers should allow you to take a motorcycle to an off-site mechanic or allow you to bring in a mechanic to inspect the bike. They won't encourage this, and they won't advertise this fact, but if you show you're serious about buying a bike, most reputable dealers will allow it.

DEALERSHIPS VERSUS THE PRIVATE SELLER

UNLESS A PRIVATE SELLER has unrealistic expectations or he or she is just fishing for a sucker to pay an inflated price, chances are that a private seller will ask less for the exact same bike than would a professional dealer. There are a number of reasons for this. A private seller isn't working on a business model that accounts for the interest he or she is paying the bank for inventory. He or she may have a loan for the bike, but most people don't think in terms of how much interest they're paying every day, as do most businesses. To make up their own financing costs, dealerships charge a little extra to help offset interest payments. They also add a certain percentage to the prices of their used bikes to cover operating costs. It costs a lot of money just to turn the lights on in a dealership every morning. Add in the salaries and health-care costs of their employees, and you can see why dealerships have to charge more for used bikes.

On the other hand, if a dealership is any good, you'll get something in return for the extra money you spend there. When buying from a private seller, the general rule is "buyer beware." After you buy a bike from a private seller, if something is wrong with it and the seller won't make it right, your only recourse may be to sue the seller, which will end up costing you even more money with no guarantee that you'll be successful.

Most shops, however, offer some sort of warranty, and if they want to have your repeat business, they'll bend over backward to make certain you are happy with your new bike. They may even be required to make it right for you by law; some states have lemon laws that apply to motorcycle dealerships as well as automobile dealerships.

If your bike does need repair, even if it's for something that happened after you bought it, dealers tend to take care of their customers. They'll be more motivated to help out a loyal customer whom they know than they will be to help out some stranger who bought a bike from a private seller. Also consider that if a dealership originally sold the bike when it was new, which is often the case with good shops that have a lot of repeat customers, chances are they'll know your bike's entire service history and will be familiar with its idiosyncrasies.

If you buy a motorcycle that still has time remaining on its factory warranty, you may be able to use the warranty to defray the cost of necessary repairs. (Be sure to check the terms of the warranty to ensure the repair is covered.) If you've bought your bike from a dealership, any dealership worthy of your business will take care of arranging for the repair and filling out warranty paperwork. If you bought your bike from a private party and take it in for warranty repairs, you may find that the dealership is not quite as helpful. That might not seem fair, but that's just the way it is.

If you need to finance your motorcycle, a dealership will have a department that does nothing but arrange financing for motorcycles. It will also be able to help you deal with all the other legal paperwork involved with buying a motorcycle, like paying sales tax, getting insurance, filling out your registration, and transferring the title. When you buy from a private seller, you'll have to deal with all these details yourself.

A good dealership will inspect, service, and check to make certain every motorcycle it sells is roadworthy; the odds are that the used bikes a good shop is selling will be reliable. The same holds true for a good private owner. A responsible owner will keep his or her motorcycle in good repair. The trick is deciding whether or not a shop or individual is reputable, and it's a lot easier to determine if a shop that sells hundreds of motorcycles every year is reputable than it is to determine the trustworthiness of a private seller who sells a bike maybe once every five or six years.

GETTING DOWN TO BUSINESS

REGARDLESS OF HOW DIFFERENT motorcycles may seem, at their hearts they are more or less all the same. After spending an entire chapter discussing the different types of bikes, this might seem like a contradiction, but when it comes to inspecting a used motorcycle, the process is pretty much the same for everything from a 250-cc single-cylinder trail bike to an 1800-cc six-cylinder Gold Wing.

In addition to a mechanic (or at least a friend who's knowledgeable about motorcycles), you'll want to bring the following items when you go to look at a used bike:

- Flashlight for looking into dark places
- Tire pressure gauge to avoid a flat while on a test ride
- Clean rag to wipe off the inevitable grease you will get on yourself
- Mechanic's mirror to see hard-to-reach items like the wiring harness

The following procedures apply to all bikes, as does the following advice: if something doesn't check out, move on and find another bike. Unless you have a mechanic estimate the costs of repairing any problems you might find, you can assume the costs will be high. Even routine maintenance like valve adjustments or tire replacement can cost hundreds of dollars. Serious repairs, like fixing a failing transmission, will cost thousands. If you pay $4,500 for a nine-year-old Yamaha Road Star with 59,000 miles, then have to drop another $3,000 fixing the transmission, you're getting dangerously close to the cost of a two-year-old carry-over version of the same bike with zero miles. (A "carry-over" is a brand-new bike from a previous season that has gone unsold.)

To keep this manageable, we'll group the parts of the bike together as follows:

- Cosmetic—This refers to the condition of the bodywork and the condition of the metal parts.
- Electrics—This will refer to the charging system, lights, battery, starter, instrumentation, and ignition.
- Chassis—For our purposes, this will include the frame itself and the bearings and bushings associated with the frame as well as the shocks, swingarm, fork, steering head, and wheels and tires.
- Drivetrain—Here we'll examine the engine, transmission, and final drive.

You can break the inspection process down into two sections—the macroscopic inspection and the microscopic inspection.

THE COSMETIC EVALUATION

THE MACROSCOPIC IS THE broad cosmetic overview of the bike, which is really a fancy way of saying your first impression of the machine.

Does It Shine?
Is the bike clean? Is it obviously well maintained? Does it have rusted metal or oxidized aluminum showing? Does is show evidence of a major crash?

Does it look like the owner took decent care of the motorcycle you're inspecting? If he rode it as carefully as he'd shave his own mother's legs with a straight razor, you'll be able to tell just from the bike's appearance. The bike will have a fresh coat of wax and the paint will glow. Even if the bike has a few miles under its belt, if it's been stored properly, ideally inside a garage, but if not, at least under a quality cover that breathes and doesn't trap moisture, the paint should be almost like new. Sure, there may be some minor scratches or some swirls in the finish—these sorts of things are inevitable on a motorcycle that gets ridden regularly—but overall the bike should shine.

Likewise the chrome should be polished to the point where the sun's reflection practically burns out the corneas of your eyes. It should not be rusted or pitted, and the chrome should be deep; you should be able to look down into it. If you find pitting in the chrome finish or rusty exhaust pipes, you could be looking at some expensive repairs.

Any exposed aluminum should be smooth and clean. If it has a whitish appearance, it is oxidizing. This usually occurs only when a bike has sat out in the elements for long periods of time (although it can occur more quickly in areas near oceans, where saltwater spray can get on a bike and degrade its metal parts). Replacing oxidized aluminum parts like engine cases and fork legs is prohibitively expensive and often exceeds the value of a motorcycle, even a Harley-Davidson. It can also be a sign that there are deeper problems with a bike, since the same elements that degraded the aluminum parts will have compromised other parts, like electrical components and rubber seals.

You may find corrosion on the metal parts around the battery box. This might look like hell, but usually it is just cosmetic, caused by an overheated battery puking out a bit of battery acid because it was overcharged. Or it had a blocked vent hose, or the battery cracked at some point. It's difficult (if not impossible) to remove this scarring, but as long as it appears to have been an isolated occurrence, it shouldn't cause any long-term harm. If it appears to be a repeated event, however, it might indicate a more serious problem with an electrical system that overcharges the battery.

On many Japanese bikes, you might find that the exposed aluminum parts have taken on a yellowish appearance, especially on older bikes. This is because they're coated with a protective film that takes on a tint as it ages. The brownish-yellow tint isn't pretty, but it's common and doesn't indicate deeper problems beyond age.

What Do Dents Mean?

Be sure to look for dents and other signs of crashing. A small ding on an exhaust pipe, footpeg tip, or clutch lever likely means a bike has fallen over, but that isn't necessarily a deal breaker. Motorcycles are inherently unstable machines, and as such they are prone to falling over. Sooner or later, every bike will fall over. A kickstand will sink into the asphalt on a hot day, or you might hit a slick patch of diesel while rolling up to a gas pump just as you happen to be crossing a rough seam in the pavement. Shit happens. The vast majority of these parking-lot tip overs result in such minor cosmetic damage that it's not worth fixing, but they do leave telltale marks on the machine.

Also, don't worry about stone chips on the fenders or the frame behind the front wheel. This is natural wear and tear and is unavoidable if the bike is to be ridden in the real world. The only bikes without stone chips are brand-new ones sitting on showroom floors or useless trailer queens hauled from bike show to bike show. All of my bikes have fallen over more than once, and each of them have pitted chrome and paint from rocks and road debris. If you ride forty thousand miles or more each year, your bikes will be pitted too.

Bigger dents are usually signs of more serious crashes that can have more dire consequences to the motorcycle's structural integrity. If a bike took a hit that was hard enough to put a grapefruit-sized divot in the gas tank, chances are the parts that you can't see took a hard hit, too. At the very least it indicates that the owner didn't treat his or her bike with the respect it deserved.

If a bike has plastic bodywork like a fairing, saddlebags, or a trunk, even a minor tip over can have much more expensive consequences. Check to make sure that all the gaps in the body panels have a uniform fit and all the tabs holding the parts together are intact and not broken off. Examine all the plastic for cracks. Even if the plastic isn't cracked, spiderweb cracks in the paint around mounting bolts are a sign that the bike has been through some sort of traumatic event. This will also show up in the metal mounting brackets that hold the bodywork in place.

Visually inspect all the plastic pieces to ensure they line up straight; if they sit crooked, something underneath them is probably bent, which could be a very bad thing.

Even if the plastic pieces appear straight, examine the brackets holding them in place (at least the ones you can see) to make sure they aren't bent or tweaked. Even if the brackets are straight, examine them for evidence that they have been straightened. This is a sign that the bike has been in a serious crash.

Check the seat cover for rips and tears. The stitching should line up, and everything should be straight. If the seat cover doesn't line up with the rest of the bike, chances are it's an aftermarket seat cover. Again, if the seat looks okay and is comfortable, this shouldn't be a deal breaker—a previous owner may have simply hooked the original seat cover with his boot and ripped it—but it could also be a sign that a motorcycle has been in a serious crash and has been rebuilt.

Most important, does the bike match the owner's description? If the seller claimed the bike was in mint condition, does it really look like it just rolled off the showroom floor, or is there oil weeping out of the head gasket? Does the bike look like it has a lot more miles than the odometer suggests? This may mean that the owner tampered with the odometer, or else that the bike spent a good part of its life sitting out in the elements even when it wasn't running. Either way, this is not good. A little exaggeration on the owner's part is to be expected, but if there is a gross discrepancy, you have no choice but to question the owner's honesty in general. If the owner has grossly misrepresented the bike, you can either negotiate the price downward or, better yet, go find a better motorcycle.

Sometimes a bike might look like it has a lot more miles on it than it really does, but in reality, it just has a lot of years under its belt. As I mentioned earlier, many riders rarely take their motorcycles out of the garage. If you just ride to town once or twice a month, you'll be lucky to put on more than four hundred miles per year. That means you can have a ten-year-old motorcycle with three or four thousand miles or less on the clock. Harleys seem especially prone to spending more time in garages than out on highways.

The end result can be a bike that might not have many miles on its odometer but is still a ten-year-old motorcycle, with ten-year-old seals and ten-year-old bearings. Harleys seem more susceptible to this sort of rot than other brands. Harleys with low miles but lots of years usually have very dry gaskets that leak motor oil everywhere. Not only should you avoid buying one of these, but you should avoid parking them in your driveway.

A PART-BY-PART GUIDE TO INSPECTING A USED MOTORCYCLE

ONCE A BIKE HAS passed the macroscopic examination, it's time to put it under the microscope. You would think a bike that looks good on the outside would be good on the inside; after all, an owner who treated a bike's cosmetics with respect should treat its mechanicals with respect, too. In most cases, you'd be correct. An owner who puts the effort into maintaining a bike's appearance usually puts as much effort into maintaining its mechanical parts. But there are always exceptions to every rule, and when you are paying your hard-earned money for a motorcycle, you don't want to pay even more because you ended up with one of those exceptions.

When buying a bike, you'll be able to put all the things you learned about the parts of a motorcycle in chapter 1 to good use. If you need to, go back and skim over that chapter to refresh your memory regarding the different systems and subsystems of a motorcycle, because you'll be examining each of them when checking out the parts of a used bike you're thinking about buying.

The Electrics
Electrical systems have historically been the weakest parts of motorcycles and the most prone to failure. This is partly because there's just not enough space to package a heavy-duty electrical system like you'd find on a car. For most of the 110 or so years that motorcycles have been manufactured, the manufacturers' solution to the problem was to keep electrical systems as simple as possible. On the earliest bikes the electrical system consisted of a crude magneto that provided spark; if the bike had any lights at all, they'd be powered by kerosene. The earliest electrical lights were powered by batteries, just like your flashlight, and as with your flashlight, those batteries had

to be replaced when they ran down. This is called a "total loss" system.

The earliest regenerating electrical systems used six-volt DC generators to charge batteries and power lights. These systems could remain crude because they didn't need to be more sophisticated; the single most difficult task of riding—starting a motorcycle—was done with legs of the flesh-and-blood kind rather than of the electrical variety. When the riding public began to demand electric starters on their motorcycles, these systems were no longer adequate and were replaced with twelve-volt systems that used automotive-style alternators to provide electrical power. By the time electronic ignition became common on bikes in the late 1970s and early 1980s, relatively reliable alternators provided all electrical power.

The slow evolution of motorcycle electrical systems is one good reason to avoid buying older bikes. Even newer bikes with early electronic ignition systems can be riddled with expensive electrical problems. For example, Yamahas from the early 1980s tended to have electrical systems that would overcharge, cooking batteries and voltage regulators. Worse yet, the Maxim 750 and 1100, a couple of Yamaha's bigger four-cylinder bikes, had crude computerized ignition systems that, when they failed, would make a bike completely inoperable. And they did fail, all the time. The system was virtually unusable and Yamaha abandoned it after just a couple of years. Yamaha is notorious for not carrying replacement parts for a motorcycle after it is out of production, meaning that within a few years, replacement computers for these bikes were virtually unobtainable. As a result, you still might run across a Yamaha Maxim 750 or 1100 or a 750 Seca that appears to be in almost new condition. Beware and avoid these bikes at all costs.

Throughout the history of motorcycles, really lousy bikes like this do crop up, sometimes from the least likely sources. For example, the four-cylinder Honda 1200-cc Gold Wings from the 1980s had a tendency to burn out their stators, which are roughly the equivalent of automotive alternators. This would have been bad enough by itself, but Honda made the matter worse by placing the stator inside the engine cases. This means to replace a stator, you'll have to split the engine cases. This is the most extensive operation you can perform on a modern Japanese motorcycle engine. It's also the most expensive one; replacing the stator on a 1200-cc Gold Wing can easily cost you $2,000–$3,000, which is close to the value of the entire bike.

As motorcycle technology advanced, bad designs like these became increasingly rare, which further underscores my point that modern motorcycles are your best bets when considering used machines. The worst electrical problem you're likely to encounter when buying a modern motorcycle is a weak battery. Modern batteries can last for years, but some climates can make them wear out more quickly. Both cold and heat can shorten the life of a battery. If a battery's not properly cared for in northern climates, they can wear out during the winter months, and in hot climates, the sun and heat can shorten a battery's life. I live in Arizona, where I replace my battery every two years just to be safe.

As good as modern electrical systems are, you'll still need to give the electrical system a thorough examination just to be safe. This is easier said than done, however, because most of the parts are buried deep within the motorcycle. Some things are easy to check, like whether or not the lights and horn work, but other things are going to take more work.

Take the wiring harness, most of which runs along the frame, or even through it; it would be damned hard to examine an entire wiring harness without completely dismantling a motorcycle, but you should make sure that at least the parts of the harness that you can see are in good shape. Big chunks of black friction tape around some section of the wiring harness, particularly up by the steering head area where the harness can get pinched in a bad crash, is a sign that the bike has likely had some major repairs.

Even the battery can be difficult to see on some bikes, but you should try to take a look at it because it can tell you a lot about a motorcycle. The terminals should be clean and free of corrosion, and the cables should be bolted on tightly. Most motorcycles now used sealed batteries, but if the bike you're looking at was built more than five or six years ago, it may have a refillable battery. If so, make certain that the battery water is set at the correct level.

The more accessories a bike has, the more powerful its electrical system needs to be. Be wary of bikes that have a lot of aftermarket electrical accessories, like GPS systems, heated seats and grips, stereos, and a couple of dozen driving lights. Modern bikes have reliable electrical systems, but only within reason. If your system was designed to produce a certain amount of power reliably, and then you mount accessories that draw twice as much juice as the system was designed to provide, your formerly reliable electrical system may not be very reliable at all. It's best to stick with a bike that only has the accessories with which it left the factory.

A lot of aftermarket accessories aren't a deal breaker. If you don't like them, usually they are easy to remove. If you do decide to keep them, make sure the owner knew what he or she was doing when they were installed. Make sure that they are wired properly, that the exposed connections are taped or sheathed, and that all connections are properly soldered or crimped.

You may not even consider the most important electrical accessory—the starter—an accessory, but those of us who began riding back when starting a motorcycle required a strong leg and a good boot know better. This is one accessory that needs to work properly. If the bike hasn't been run in a while or if the weather is cold, a bike you're looking at might need a little help to turn over, but once the bike has been run for a while—say thirty minutes or so out on the highway—the starter should spin the engine to life with no drama. Failure to do so might just mean that a bike needs a new battery, but it could also be a sign that a bike needs expensive repairs.

If you aren't able to take the bike out for a test ride to charge up the battery, at least check the charging indicator light. Most bikes will have some sort of idiot light (that's what we used to call indicator lights that were used when what was really needed was a good gauge) for the charging system. Although it does not provide much useful information, at the very least an idiot light lets you know when there is a problem. If the light continues to glow after the engine is running at normal idle speed, the bike either has charging problems or soon will have them.

If you do uncover anything amiss with the electrical system, my advice is to run as far and fast as you can and find another bike to buy. The problems may well be simple and inexpensive to fix, but usually they will be difficult and extremely expensive, and they'll undoubtedly be tricky to find and diagnose. If you have any doubts about your expertise in motorcycle electrics, this is one of the best reasons to have a competent professional examine the bike you're thinking about buying.

With more and more bikes using antilock brake systems (ABS), electrics also are playing an increasingly large role in brake performance. These are highly complex, computer-based systems that defy intuitive understanding. But it doesn't take a scientist to understand that brake performance can be the difference between life and death. If you look at a bike that has ABS and the brakes don't seem to perform properly, do not buy that motorcycle without having a qualified mechanic check the ABS equipment. I know that in addition to being dangerous, ABS failures are extremely expensive. I personally would not buy a bike with ABS problems.

The Chassis

You'll need a good electrical system just to get your bike out on the road, but once you're out riding, you must make sure the rest of the bike is up to par, too—particularly the frame and suspension.

I'm going to start at the front of the bike and work my way back. The most complicated system (and thus most prone to failure) is the fork. A fork is probably the most likely item to get tweaked in a crash, since it is at the front of the bike and the first thing that connects with whatever a rider might be crashing into. It is also prone to less serious problems, like worn-out seals.

The majority of motorcycles you will be looking at will use hydraulically damped telescopic forks. These are the two long shock absorbers connecting your front wheel to your handlebar. There are other types of front ends—Harley uses an old-fashioned springer-type fork on some models, and BMW has too many oddball systems to keep track of—but I'm going to focus on the hydraulic front fork, which is the most common type.

The fork assembly is held together by metal pieces called "triple clamps." These attach the fork to the steering head, which is the tubular assembly on the front of the frame in which the fork pivots. The triple clamps hold either the fork tubes or the fork sliders, depending on what type is used. Think of the fork tube as the male part of the fork, the part that inserts into the female part, and the slider as the female part that gets penetrated by the male part. (This may seem crude, but these are the terms that mechanics have always used.)

Traditionally the male part is at the top and the female part is at the bottom, but I've noticed that in recent years the trend has been to reverse these positions. Consequently, the inserting male part is now often found at the bottom, down by the wheel, and the female part is up by the triple clamps. These were originally called "upside-down forks," and are still often referred to as "USD forks," though they are becoming so common that more often than not people just call them "forks." At first USD forks were only found on sport bikes, but now they've begun to appear on all types of bikes, including cruisers. Harley uses USD forks on its new Sportster XR1200 and Victory uses them on its Hammer and Kingpin models.

The first tools you'll need to check a bike's fork are your eyeballs. Look at the fork from the side. The two legs of the fork should line up perfectly. If one of the legs is skewed at a bit of an angle or looks bent, chances are the bike has experienced more than the normal amount of wear and tear. If the whole assembly looks a little cockeyed, then either the triple clamps are bent or the frame itself is bent in such a way that the steering head itself is tweaked. In the grand scheme of things, these problems range from really bad to downright terrible, and they should motivate you to find a different bike.

The other thing to look for in the visual inspection is oil leaking from a fork seal. If the fork hasn't been cleaned, you'll easily be able to see a ring where oil has collected and grime has built up around the fork tube, right at the end of the fork slider's travel (the point at which the male part is most deeply inserted into the female part). Even if you don't see this telltale ring, the fork seals may leak; the owner may just have wiped the tubes down so the leak wasn't obvious.

You can tell if this is the case with a simple test. First, make certain that the owner or the mechanic you brought along, or anyone else capable of standing on his or her own two feet, is standing beside the bike to help keep it secure. Go to the front of the bike and get a strong grip on the handlebar. With the front wheel placed firmly between your legs, squeeze the front brake lever to keep the bike from rolling away from you (or worse yet, over you) and lift the bike up off its side stand. Once you have the bike securely upright, pump the fork up and down a few times. When you are finished, put the bike back down on its side stand, making sure that it's resting in a secure position, and rub your finger along the exposed part of the fork tube above (or below on USD forks) the slider. If the seal is leaking, you'll feel a thin film of oil.

If the bike is more than a few years old and hasn't had the fork seals replaced, there's a good chance you'll find a leaky fork seal. A leaky fork seal shouldn't be a deal breaker, but like just about everything else associated with a motorcycle, it will be relatively expensive to fix. Call a motorcycle shop that sells the model you're looking at and get a quote for replacing the seals. Your final offer for the bike should reflect the money you'll have to pay to repair the fork.

Follow the same procedure to check for other possible fork problems. When you're pumping the fork up and down, make certain that both sides of the fork legs are moving up and down freely, with-

out binding or making noise, both of which could be
signs of expensive problems to come.

Steering Head Bearings

You can check the steering head bearings at the same
time you're checking out the fork. While you're holding the bike up turn the handlebar all the way to the
left, then all the way back to the right. Listen to see if
you hear a clunking sound, which could indicate that
a steering head bearing is loose or worn out; it may
have dents and flat spots that can't be adjusted away.

If the bike has a center stand, put it up on the
center stand, as described in chapter 3.

Once the bike is securely on the stand, have the
person who's with you place his or her weight on
the rear of the bike. This should lift the front tire in
the air. When you've made sure the bike is secure,
center the bar so that the tire is facing straight ahead
and let it fall to one side, and then the other. If the
wheel moves evenly and smoothly, chances are it's
in good condition. If it moves with a clunky, jerky
motion, the bike likely has problems with the steering head bearings.

Again, this is not uncommon on older bikes, and
it shouldn't be a deal breaker; the bearings may just
need an adjustment, but there is a good chance that
they will need to be replaced. This will be even more
expensive than leaky fork seals, especially if the bike
has a lot of bodywork that needs to be removed. Check
with a local shop to find out what this will cost to
repair, and if you decide to buy the bike, make an offer
that will reflect that cost.

While you have the front of the bike up in the air, check the condition of the wheel bearings by grasping the front wheel at a right angle to the fork and rock it from side to side. If you notice any play in the wheel, the wheel bearing will need shimming or replacement.

Tires

If you're used to automobile tires, which often last fifty thousand miles or more, you're in for a rude and expensive awakening when it comes to motorcycle tires. The very best motorcycle tires won't last ten thousand miles; in most cases you'll be doing good to get seventy-five hundred miles from a set of tires. And these tires are expensive; on big touring bikes like the Gold Wing or Vision that require the removal of a lot of plastic bodywork to gain access to the tires, you could be looking at $600-plus to buy a set of high-quality tires, and another $300 to have a shop mount them.

There's really no way around this—it's just the price you'll pay to ride a motorcycle—but with that said, you can still do a few things to help keep your costs down, even when you first buy a bike. Pick up a tread-measuring tool and measure the depth of the tread on any bike you're thinking of buying. Make sure the tires have at least 50 percent of their tread life left. If they don't, get an estimate for the cost of tire replacement from your local shop and reflect those costs in any offer you might make for the bike.

Check the air pressure of the tires. Low air pressure is obviously not a major problem, but you'll want to make certain that the tires are properly inflated before a bike is safe to take out on a test ride (consult the owner's manual for the proper air-pressure level). Low pressure can mean a tire has a leak, but as often as not it just means the bike might have sat unused for a while. If a bike has been unused for more than a few months, check the sidewalls for dry rot, cracks, and weather checking. If a tire shows signs of problems like this, it should be replaced regardless of how much tread is left on it.

You can get a lot of information from the tire itself, like the date the tire was manufactured, for example. The date of manufacture is found in the final four-digit code stamped into the small oval area on the tire's sidewall, right after the word *DOT* (Department of Transportation). The first two digits denote the week of the year in which the tire was manufactured and the last two digits represent the last two numbers of the year of manufacture. For example, if a tire was manufactured in June of 2006, the code will read: "2806."

If the tire has a code that ends in three digits, that means the tire was manufactured before the year 2000. If that's the case, then figure that you will need to replace it regardless of how good it looks. There is no hard-and-fast rule about how old a tire should get before replacing, but if you don't have the sense not to ride on tires that are over ten years old, you should probably take up a safer hobby, like knitting. Even if a tire is just six or seven years old, you can assume it's past its prime and will need replacement before you start riding the bike. Again, this isn't a deal breaker, but when negotiating to buy the bike, your offer should reflect the cost of tire replacement.

Frames

Modern motorcycle frames are generally pretty robust pieces of equipment and won't shake to pieces the way they used to on earlier bikes. (There are, however, exceptions, including Suzuki's first-generation TL1000, a high-performance V-twin sport bike built in the late 1990s and early 2000s, and which developed a notable reputation for frame failure. Most frames you look at will either be made of tubular steel or aluminum alloy beams, though those found on BMWs from the 1980s and 1990s are virtually not frames at all, but rather consist of a couple of subframes bolted to the engine cases. In general, these were strong and reliable and should be no more problematic than the frames on other modern bikes.

Even though frame failures are rare, you should still take some time to inspect the frame of any used bike you consider buying. Check the gussets and welds for cracks, especially in high-stress areas like around the steering head. Look for dents or severe scratches that might indicate a bike has been wrecked, and look for signs of corrosion around the battery box. Take note of flaking paint, which could also be a sign that a bike has been through a serious crash. Don't walk away from a bike because of a little flaking in the frame's paint, but if you do see this, keep your eyes open for other trouble signs.

Swingarms/Rear Suspensions

All modern motorcycles have some sort of swinging arm rear suspension. From the 1950s until the 1980s this consisted of a fairly standard setup, with a metal fork attached to the rear wheel, coming together in front of the wheel, and attaching to the frame at a pivot point behind the transmission. A pair of shocks, one on either side of the rear wheel, controlled the wheel's up-and-down motion.

This status quo began to change in the mid-1970s. Yamaha used the first modern single-shock setup on its factory motocross race bike in 1973. Within a few years both Yamaha and Suzuki offered single-shock dirt bikes to the general public. At first these used triangular swingarms that placed the shock at the top of the triangle, in front of the rear tire. The shocks on these bikes rested at an angle and connected to the frame up under the gas tank. This system was soon replaced by a setup that placed the shock upright in front of the wheel. By the early 1980s all competitive dirt bikes used this latter setup.

At the same time, single-shock arrangements began to appear on street bikes. In 1980 BMW introduced the R80G/S, an 800-cc dual sport that featured a single shock, though this was mounted in the traditional position, alongside the rear wheel. Where the BMW design broke with tradition was its use of a single-sided rear swingarm, which was basically like a traditional swingarm cut in half. BMW called this system the "Monolever."

Yamaha used a more innovative single-shock system when it introduced the Virago series in 1981. These early Yamahas used a system much like the very first single-shock dirt bikes, with a triangular swingarm and a laid-down shock that ran under the seat and connected to the frame up by the gas tank.

Over the next few years Japanese sport bikes began to feature single-shock rear suspensions, though these followed the practice of the later dirt bikes, with a vertical shock mounted in front of the rear tire. Harley even got into the alternative rear suspension business with its Softail system. Like the Virago, this system featured a triangular rear swingarm, but instead of being located under the seat, the shocks were mounted down under the engine, hidden from sight.

The main difference between the Harley system and the various systems used by the Japanese and Germans was that the Japanese and German systems were all about function. The main purpose of the Harley system was cosmetic; Harley was trying to re-create the look of the earlier hardtails (bikes without any rear suspension at all). It did this by hiding the entire rear suspension system as best it could.

Today we have a bewildering variety of rear suspension designs to pick from. Having said all this, unless you're planning to spend a lot of time on a racetrack, you should simply make sure that any used bike you're buying doesn't have problems with its swingarm. Swingarms generally are extremely stout and should cause little trouble over the life of a motorcycle, but you'll still need to check for potential problems.

First, examine the shock or shocks. Make sure they aren't leaking fluid, or that they haven't lost their gas charge if they are nitrogen shocks. You can check for leaks in much the same way you check the fork seals—bounce the bike up and down and then check for greasy moisture on the shaft of the shock. You should be able to tell if the shocks are properly charged and/or filled with fluid after you bounce the bike up and down. If it bounces too easily, the shock(s) will probably need work. This is not uncommon on bikes with a few miles under their belts, but like everything else, it will be expensive.

An even more expensive repair would be to replace the swingarm pivot bushings. When these get bad, they can make your rear wheel wobble while you ride down the road. As you might imagine, this can have fatal consequences on the highway and needs to be fixed immediately. Thankfully you should easily be able to determine if the swingarm bushings are bad before your bike enters a "death wobble" on the open road. The procedure for checking swingarm bushings is similar to checking the steering head bearing and is much easier to do on a bike equipped with a center stand. When the bike is on a center stand, the rear wheel is lifted up in the air so you can wiggle it back and forth to see if there is any play in the bushings. If there is a little play, that might not mean there's a problem—on many bikes the swingarm pivot simply can be adjusted to eliminate this play—but if the swingarm clunks from side to side, you can be certain the bike will soon experience expensive and dangerous problems. Walk away from any bike with a sick swingarm while you still can.

The Final Drive

This is also the time to check the final drive system. As mentioned in chapter 1, there are three common types of final drive systems: chains, shafts, and belts. Belts are the best system, in my opinion, and require little maintenance, but they can fail with age and wear. For this reason, check the condition of the rubber to ensure it's not cracked or coming apart. Most important, make certain the belt has all of its teeth. If teeth are missing from the belt, it is just about to fail.

A damaged belt is not a huge problem on some belt-drive bikes, but, on others, it could get expensive. Generally speaking, if the belt runs inside the frame as it passes over the swingarm pivot between the front and rear pulleys, as it does on Harley-Davidson touring bikes and Softail models, the frame will have to come apart to replace the belt. This is a huge job and is much more expensive than changing belts on models that have the belt running outside the frame, such as Harley's Dyna and Sportster models. If the belt has any damage or noticeable wear, check with a local shop to see how much they charge for replacing belts on that model. If you decide to buy the bike, reflect the cost of belt replacement in your offer.

I prefer belts over shafts because belts don't alter the handling characteristics of a bike the way shafts do, even though shafts require less maintenance than belts. When you have a shaft-driven bike up on a center stand (most bikes with shaft drives have center stands), you can check the oil level in the rear drive unit by opening a screw-in plug that rests on the upper part of the ring and pinion housing and looking inside to see that the oil is at the proper level. Once you've determined that it is, put the bike in gear (with the engine off, of course), grab the rear wheel, and jerk it back and forth. If you feel a loud, loose "clunk" inside the rear drive housing, the bike may be about to experience a very expensive drive-shaft failure.

Chains are the most common types of rear-drive systems, and they also wear out the fastest. In the 1970s and early 1980s a few manufacturers like Harley-Davidson and Yamaha used chain-drive systems that ran the chain in an enclosed oil bath. These enclosed chains lasted virtually forever, but the cases that held the oil were heavy and prone to leaking. They eventually proved to be a technologi-cal dead end and by the mid-1980s all motorcycle companies had abandoned the idea and gone back to open chains and sprockets, or in Harley's case, belts.

You'd be lucky to get twenty thousand miles from a chain and a set of sprockets. If you're like me, that won't get you through one riding season. Add to that the fact that the chain final drive is the most maintenance-intensive system on a modern motorcy-cle, and you can see why I don't care for them. You'll need to adjust your chain at least every week, perhaps every other day if you're a serious rider.

Be prepared to get dirty when checking the con-dition of the chain. Although there are some good chain lubricants that don't leave a greasy buildup or attract too much road grime, even the cleanest chain on a bike that is regularly ridden will be somewhat greasy and dirty. This is where the clean rag you brought along will come in handy.

First check the tension on the chain to make certain the chain isn't so loose that it will cause problems when riding. If the bike is well maintained, then the slack should be within the manufacturer's tolerance, usually meaning the chain should have enough free play to move up and down an inch or two. An overly tight chain might be evidence of a well-meaning but ill-informed seller. A slightly loose chain may only mean the bike gets ridden a lot, but in my mind, a chain that is sloppy is a red flag indicating its owner neglects basic maintenance. If the chain is too loose to ride safely, have the owner adjust it before going out on a test ride.

When the chain tension has been set to the proper level, roll the rear wheel to turn the chain and check it at various spots. If the tension varies from location to location, the chain may have tight spots, indicating that it is on its last legs.

The condition of the sprockets will also tell you how long you can expect the chain to last. Since the wheel only turns one direction under power (no chain-driven motorcycles have reverse gears), the teeth of the sprockets only wear on one side. Because of this, they develop a distinct cupping appearance as they wear out—one side of each tooth appears worn and the other appears almost new.

Sprockets usually wear out at almost identical rates as chains, requiring the chain and both sprockets to be replaced at the same time. Since wear is much easier to see on the sprockets than on the chain itself, you can expect that the chain will have about as much life left in it as do the sprockets. If the owner claims to have replaced the chain but not the sprockets, ignore anything the person says after that because he or she is either a liar or a fool.

If the bike lacks a center stand, the process of checking the suspension and chassis gets a lot trickier. Here's where taking the bike to a mechanic can be worthwhile, because any worthy mechanic will have a lift he or she can use to hoist the bike up for these types of examinations. Barring access to a secure lift, your next best bet is to use a good stand, like those built by the company Pit Bull. Quality stands will support either wheel (if you have two, you can support both ends at once), but unlike a lift designed specifically for motorcycles, which connect to a bike at the center of the frame, stands lift a bike at its wheels. This loads the suspension with the weight of the motorcycle, making it much more difficult to check for problems with the swingarm bushings or steering head bearing.

Brakes

The brakes on any motorcycle you'll consider buying are perhaps the single most important items when it comes to saving your bacon out on the highway. There are two kinds of brakes: disc brakes and drum brakes. Disc brakes slow your motorcycle by squeezing pistons inside calipers, which are attached to your frame or fork so that they don't rotate with the wheel. These pistons push pads against a disc that's connected to the wheel so that it rotates with the wheel. The pressure of the pistons slows and gradually stops the wheel's rotation.

Drum brakes work by expanding the brake

shoes—stationary, horseshoe-shaped devices—against the inner surface of a rotating wheel hub. As mentioned earlier, you'll only run across drum brakes on extremely low-end motorcycles, usually the smallest cruisers from the Japanese manufacturers, which often still feature drum brakes in the back. The majority of quality motorcycles you'll be considering will have discs at either end.

Finding a bike you like with a drum rear brake shouldn't cause you to exclude that bike automatically. Disc brakes are unquestionably better, but drum brakes can be at least adequate, provided a motorcycle isn't too heavy. Make certain they work smoothly and stop the bike without shuddering.

If there is a problem with the rear drum brake, this means the shoes are worn. Often these can be adjusted. There will be a lever coming out of the wheel hub that activates the shoes inside. Where the lever connects to the brake cable leading to the brake pedal on the right side of the engine, there should be an adjustable rod connecting the cable to the lever. This rod will have a spring on it to keep tension between the rod and the lever. You'll find an adjustable nut at the end of the rod. If the nut is at the beginning of its travel and there is a lot of room to tighten it down before it reaches the end of its travel, chances are the brake shoes still have some usable life in them. If the nut has been adjusted down toward the end of its travel, most likely the brake shoes will need to be replaced soon.

Replacing the brake shoes is a relatively inexpensive process, and one you can easily do yourself, even if you're not mechanically inclined. The hardest part of replacing the shoes is getting the wheel off the bike. If you can do that, the brake cover should just pop off. Yet even simple tasks require your full attention to detail. Always remember that the life you are putting on the line will be your own. As you start taking the wheel apart, take careful notes, outlining where everything goes, so you can put it all back together correctly when you are finished. Leave off one cotter key or leave one bolt loose, and you might find that your wheel falls off when you stab at the brake pedal. If you have any doubts whatsoever about your ability to fix your own brakes, leave the job to a professional.

If you find a bike with a drum brake in front, it will either be too old or too small for you to seriously consider buying. Any bike worth purchasing will have at least one disc brake up front, and likely two. The process for checking disc brakes is quite a bit different than it is for drum brakes.

The first thing you need to check is the condition of the fluid. This will be in a reservoir on the handlebar, right up by the front brake lever. Some BMWs from the 1970s placed the reservoir under the tank, and custom bike builders often place reservoirs in the oddest places you can imagine. But if you're following my advice, you're not going to be looking at antiques or hand-built customs, so any bike you should be looking at will have the front brake reservoir on the right handlebar.

Check both the clarity and level of the brake fluid. The fluid should be relatively clear and set to the correct level. Generally speaking, brake fluid levels don't vary all that much on a properly functioning brake system. In hundreds of thousands of miles of riding, I've rarely had to add fluid to modern disc brakes. A low fluid level usually means there is some sort of leak in the system or that it hasn't been properly maintained and is seriously overdue for a fluid change. Either case is bad news and ought to ring alarm bells.

Likewise fluid that is cloudy or dirty-looking is a sign that something isn't right. This indicates that the bike's owner has neglected to perform routine maintenance or that the brake system is contaminated. If the fluid level is low or if the fluid itself looks murky, chances are an expensive brake repair is in the bike's near future—or worse yet, the system is on the verge of experiencing a catastrophic failure that could end with you being crippled or killed.

After checking the fluid in the front brake master cylinder, move on to the brake hoses. Make certain the visible hoses aren't cracked, kinked, or obviously leaking. If they appear to be in rough condition, it's another sign the bike has been seriously neglected.

But even hoses that look good on the outside might be worn out, especially if the bike is more than five or six years old. You'll only be able to determine this with a test ride. If the front brake lever feels mushy; if there is a slight pause between pulling the brake lever and when the brake pads start to bite into the disc; or if the brake lever seems to move too close to the handlebar, you've got a bike with problematic brakes. It may be something extremely simple, like air in the brake lines. This can be cured by bleeding the brakes. (If you don't know how to do this already, you should probably leave it to a mechanic. If the bike has ABS, then you'll definitely want to leave bleeding to a trained mechanic, even if you know how to bleed brakes yourself, because ABS systems are incredibly complicated.) On the other hand, a mushy brake lever could also indicate the need for new brake lines.

Needing new brake lines is not a major issue and shouldn't dissuade you from buying a bike. In fact, if the bike is more than five or six years old, expect to replace them sooner or later, even if they aren't causing obvious problems when you buy the bike. It's a relatively simple procedure, but like everything else related to motorcycle maintenance, it is expensive. Get an estimate and, as always, include the replacement cost in your offer.

(A side note on brakes: if you need to replace the brake lines, you should spend a few extra dollars and replace them with braided-steel lines, which will last much longer and are also much better-looking.)

Next you'll need to check the brake pads. Most brake calipers will have some sort of cap on top of them. You should be able to pop this cap off and visually inspect the pads. This consists of simply looking at the pads to see how far down the material that grabs the brake discs has worn. Generally, new pads have at least a quarter inch of material on them. Most have a groove in the middle of the pads that runs almost all the way through the material. You can use that groove as a gauge to determine how far the pads have worn down.

Worn brake pads really aren't an issue when buying a used bike because pads are relatively easy and cheap to replace. The most expensive pads on the market seldom cost more than $50, and if you change the pads yourself, you'll save hundreds of dollars over the cost of having the pads replaced in a shop. The first step is usually to remove the calipers by unfastening the two bolts that hold them to the caliper carriers. (On some bikes you don't even have to do this—you can replace the pads with the calipers in place.) Then you pop the inspection cover off, remove a couple of pins, and remove the pads. Putting in the new pads is just a little more difficult, because you'll have to press the pistons back into the calipers to make room for the new pads, which will be much thicker than the old ones due to their additional pad material. This might require using a little force.

Be aware that the pistons are easily damaged. If you try to pry them apart with a metal tool, you'll likely damage the metal on the pistons, creating sharp edges that can tear seals and cause costly leaks. You'll need something soft, like a wood stick, to safely pry apart the pistons. After that, you should be able to drop the calipers in, replace the pins (along with the clips or keys that secure the pins in place), and you're done. Again, if you're going to replace the brake pads yourself, as with any repair, make certain you take careful notes and put everything back together properly. No helmet, riding jacket, boots, gloves, or any other protective gear will save you if your brake calipers fall off. Because of this, if you have any doubts at all about your ability to change the brake pads, leave the job to a professional.

The last part of the brake system you'll examine will be the rotors. These will also be the easiest parts to examine, since they are usually right out in the open where you can see them. Look at them from the front or from the top, whichever gives you the best view, and make sure they're straight and not warped. Have the owner or a friend roll the bike while you look at the brakes because any warping will be more obvious while the wheel is turning.

When the bike is stationary, run your hands across the braking surfaces. The faces of the discs should feel smooth. If the bike has any miles at all on it, you'll most likely feel some ridges, but these shouldn't be numerous or deep. Damaged discs could be another sign of a crash; at the very least they're evidence of improper maintenance.

Checking the Oil

You would think that anyone selling a bike would have the sense to make certain the engine had oil, but I didn't live this long by overestimating the average person's capacity for common sense. Most people will have the oil filled to the proper level, but you don't want to have an engine seize up and cause you to crash because you happened across the one idiot who didn't.

Most modern motorcycles use wet-sump oil systems. These are similar to automotive systems in that the oil is held in a reservoir at the bottom of the crankcase and is checked via a dipstick.

However, unlike automotive dipsticks, which are usually held in place by rubber plugs and their own weight, motorcycle dipsticks are usually made of lightweight plastic and screwed in place. This can lead to confusion when checking the oil, since some manufacturers require you to screw the dipstick all the way down to check the level while others require you to unscrew it and simply let it rest in the filler hole to get the proper level. The difference between these two methods is significant and can lead to underfilling, or worse yet, overfilling the oil reservoir by as much as one quart. The only way to find out for certain which method you need to use is to check the owner's manual (any conscientious owner will have an owner's manual to go with a bike—if he or she doesn't, you should probably find another bike).

If a bike has a center stand, place the bike on the stand to check the oil level. On bikes that lack center stands, you'll have to consult the owner's manual to find out whether you should check the oil with the bike on its side stand or if you need to have someone hold the bike upright while you check the oil. You'd think that manufacturers who neglected to fit bikes with center stands would design their dipsticks to work with the bike on its side stand, but you'd be wrong most of the time. More often than not you'll have to figure out a way to hold the bike upright to check oil, which is a major pain in the ass and very unsafe if you don't have a stand or have someone to help you.

While you're checking the oil level, check the condition of the oil. It should be relatively clear and brown. The blacker and dirtier it is, the longer it's been since the oil was changed. In addition to being sludgy and dirty, old oil doesn't provide adequate lubrication. The job of the oil is to coat the moving metal parts with a thin film so that the metal moves on the oil film rather than having metal rub against metal.

Oil is classified in two categories: organic and synthetic. Organic oil is the black stuff that is pumped out of the ground. Synthetic oil is man-made and is better in just about every respect than organic oil. Organic oil starts to break down after a thousand or so miles of use; synthetic oil doesn't start to break down until two thousand miles of use. When the molecules in oil start to break down, oil loses its ability to evenly coat the metal with a layer of film, leading to metal-on-metal contact, which is what makes an engine wear out.

Because of this, you'll want to change oil at least every two thousand to three thousand miles if you use organic oil. I use organic oil and change it every twenty-five hundred miles. If you run synthetic oil, you can go three thousand to four thousand miles between oil changes. Many manufacturers specify oil changes at six thousand to eight thousand miles, but this is just marketing hype. My coauthor, Darwin Holmstrom, once asked Erik Buell, former president of the late Buell Motorcycle Company, about this. Buell is a straight shooter and answered honestly. "Of course anyone who knows anything about engines won't go any longer than four thousand miles without changing oil on any bike," he said, "but the other manufacturers still recommend longer intervals for marketing reasons. We have to play their game."

If the oil is black and dirty-looking, then it's gone longer than three thousand to four thousand miles between oil changes. This means that the engine has experienced abnormal wear. Modern engines are tough and will take a certain amount of abuse, so if everything checks out on the bike (and it doesn't have very many miles on the clock), then you still might consider buying one with dirty oil, but I'd probably find another bike. Changing oil is the most basic routine maintenance you can perform on a bike. If an owner has neglected this, he or she has probably neglected everything else, too.

When you examine the oil, smell it. A burnt smell indicates serious engine problems and should cause you to move on to another bike. Also look for specs of crud in the oil. These could be metal shavings and indicate a serious problem. If the bike is barely broken in, you might find a few small metal shavings in the oil, an indication that it left the factory with tolerances that might have been on the tight side, but if the bike is well broken in, metal shavings in the oil are bad news.

In liquid-cooled bikes, also watch for any creamy froth on top of the oil. This indicates a leaking head gasket that allows antifreeze into the oil, which means the bike will need extensive repairs before it's safe and reliable to ride. If you see evidence of this on the dipstick, thank the owner for taking the time to show you the bike and move on to the next bike.

THE ROAD TEST

AT THIS POINT YOU'LL have learned about as much as you can from examining a stationary bike. If a used motorcycle meets your standards up until here, you'll have to take it for a road test to determine whether the engine and transmission are up to snuff. I know you'll likely want to get straight to the road test, which is by far the most fun part of the entire process, but there's a reason you save this for last—you need to check out everything else to make certain the bike is safe to ride before you risk your life by taking it out on the road.

Although the road test may be exciting for the buyer, it's the least enjoyable for the seller. A dealership might not let you ride a bike at all, though they are more likely to let you ride a used bike than a new one. The dealer may tell you that you won't be able to ride the bike because of insurance reasons, but if you can convince the dealer you're seriously considering buying the bike, you should be able to talk the salesperson into a test ride. It helps if you look like a potentially serious buyer. This is one time it pays to dress conservatively; if you have tribal tattoos on your forehead and are wearing a T-shirt that says "Fuck Death!" your odds of getting a test ride diminish considerably.

Even a private seller may be reluctant to let you ride his or her motorcycle. You can hardly blame the owner; the person is trying to get money by selling his or her bike. To get the most money for the bike, the person likely has worked hard to make it as presentable as possible. Should some dimwit take the bike on a test ride and drop it, the owner loses.

The seller can't count on the potential buyer to do the right thing if a mishap occurs on a test drive; that is, financially compensate the seller for any potential damage to the bike. If that happens, the seller may have to show the bike to an insurance company, which will probably require the seller to pay some sort of deductible, and then the company may jack up his or her rates. So, although you really should ride any bike you are considering buying, don't be surprised if the seller requires some sort of written agreement or security deposit before he or she lets you take out the bike. It might be a bit of an overreaction, but it is understandable.

You should always treat a motorcycle with respect, and this is especially true when that motorcycle belongs to someone else. You're not trying to see how fast the motorcycle is—there are dozens of magazines and websites with professionals who have already answered that question for you. And you're not trying to prove you're the next road-racing superstar. You're just trying to determine the mechanical soundness of the bike.

In addition to confirming the quality of the frame and suspension, the focus of your road test should be to determine the condition of the engine and transmission. If you think the other stuff is expensive, check out the cost of an engine or transmission rebuild in a modern motorcycle. Chances are the costs could approach what you pay for the motorcycle in the first place.

ONCE YOU'VE DETERMINED THAT THE BIKE has the proper amount of oil and that the oil is in good condition, start the engine and let it warm up—trying to ride a motorcycle with a cold engine won't tell you much more about it than that the engine is cold.

If the bike has a center stand, leave it on the stand while warming up. When the bike is on the side stand, the oil will slosh to one side of the oil pan. Depending on the position of the pickup of the oil pump, if the oil sloshes too far to one side of the pan or the other, the pump might suck air instead of oil, especially if the oil level is low. Because of this, some bikes, especially older Japanese four cylinders, can starve the top ends of oil if they are run for extended periods while resting on their side stands. (This won't be a problem if the bike has a dry-sump system like that used by Harley-Davidson.)

Once you're out on the road, pay attention to the overall feel of the motorcycle. Does the frame feel solid or does it squirm around underneath you? Does the suspension seem controlled, yet compliant? Or is it soft and mushy? Or perhaps stiff and bouncing? Does the bike track straight or does it move down the road like it's a crab? Do all the controls work properly or are they sticky and stiff? For the most part you're looking for surprises, since you should have a handle on all of these areas from your earlier inspection of the bike.

You're not going to be pushing a bike's handling limits on a test ride, but you will want to get a feel for the general soundness of the chassis. The bike should track straightly and predictably when pointed down the road, corner without any drama, and be stable on the straights. The suspension should be firm but compliant. The fork shouldn't dive excessively during braking and the rear shock(s) shouldn't bottom out over bumps. Make certain the bike doesn't shake its head when decelerating, particularly in the 45- to 30-mile-per-hour range. If it does, it may just need a steering head bearing adjustment, or the bike may just have mismatched tires (this is easy enough to check once you've stopped), but a bearing replacement is probably in the cards.

The main things you're checking on the test ride are the engine and transmission. A strong engine should start easily and idle smoothly once warmed up. An uneven idle could indicate problems with the carburetors or fuel-injection system. The bike should accelerate without hesitation and should not miss or pop. It most definitely should not produce any smoke from the exhaust pipe once the engine is warmed up, and you shouldn't smell a strong odor of unburned gasoline. If you see white smoke, the engine is burning oil. If you see black smoke, the bike is running rich, meaning it's getting too much gas and not enough air in the fuel charge. Either way, it's not good. Any hiccups, uneven response, or engine bogging indicates a fuel-delivery system problem.

The engine shouldn't make any ticking, rattling, or other mechanical knocking sounds. All you should hear is the burble of the exhaust. Some engines emit a whining sound from their cam gears, especially some of the gear-driven V-fours from Honda, but this shouldn't sound like something inside the engine is broken.

The transmission should pop into first gear with slick mechanical precision; there should be no clunks, reluctance, or any other drama. Clutch take-up should be progressive. If the clutch is jerky and sudden, it could just mean that the clutch cable needs to be adjusted, or it could mean that the clutch itself is weak. If this seems like a problem, have the owner adjust the clutch cable per the procedure outlined in the owner's manual and see if that takes care of the problem. If it doesn't, you need to be suspicious of the clutch. This might also indicate potentially expensive transmission problems.

The rest of the shifts should be as smooth and slick as the shift into first gear. Pay special attention to any clunky shifts or grinding noises coming from the transmission, especially on Yamahas. For years, from the mid-1980s until at least the early 2000s, some Yamahas were prone to transmission failure, the result of Yamaha's practice of using tolerances that were too loose in their transmissions. Most of the afflicted bikes will have had their transmissions fail by now and will have been rebuilt to tighter tolerances, and a lot of people have ridden tens of thousands of miles with no problems at all. Even if I didn't have a policy of buying American-built motorcycles, I'd still stay away from used Yamahas.

But any motorcycle can have a bad transmission. For example, Harley's early five-speed transmissions—those built before the late 1980s—had notoriously weak shifting forks and were prone to expensive failures. This problem was so prevalent that it opened the door for a lot of aftermarket transmission builders like Baker, most of whom made transmissions that were as good as (and, more often than not, better than) the original equipment trannies that Harley used.

When Harley switched to six-speed transmissions in 2008, they once again had transmission problems. They had really bad fifth gears that would fail. It turned out that the problem was caused by the way the fifth gear was cut. Harley revised the way it cut the fifth-gear cogs for 2009 and the problem seems to have gone away.

If you suspect any problems at all with the transmission, pay close attention and don't buy the bike unless you are sure that the problem was something like a loose clutch cable or a poor shift on your part and not with the transmission itself. If a bike pops out of gear, head directly back to the owner and give the bike back to him or her before the transmission fails completely, possibly giving an unscrupulous seller an opening to blame you for the failed transmission. And a bike that pops out of gear will have its transmission fail sooner rather than later. You don't even need to call a shop and find out what a transmission rebuild will cost you, because I can answer that question for you: too damned much.

When you get the bike into top gear out on the road—roughly at 45 miles per hour on most bikes—accelerate up to the speed limit. The engine's rpm should rise in proportion to your speed. If the engine seems to spool up faster than you're building speed, the clutch is probably slipping.

Replacing the clutch isn't all that expensive compared to transmissions. But consider that modern clutches are pretty tough, so if the clutch is wearing out on a bike that doesn't have a lot of miles, chances are that it's been seriously abused, perhaps even raced. A weak clutch should serve as a warning flag for other potential problems.

What You Should Know

- A thorough inspection up front can save you thousands of dollars down the road.
- When in doubt, consult a good mechanic.
- If something doesn't check out, find another motorcycle.

CHAPTER FIVE

BUYING A BIKE

Like most aspects of motorcycle ownership, the process of buying bikes is different from automobiles—you'll find this out as soon as you go to finance and insure your bike. Whether you buy a new bike or a used bike, you'll need to make a few arrangements before you ride home on your new (or new-to-you) machine. As mentioned in the last chapter, if you buy a bike from a dealership, the staff can help you with details like financing, licensing, and insurance; but if you're buying a used bike from a private seller, you'll have to arrange for these things yourself. Either way, you'll want to keep in mind some important considerations that are unique to buying bikes.

PRICING A USED MOTORCYCLE

DETERMINING WHAT'S A FAIR value for any used motorcycle you're looking at will be a challenge. There are
online resources like the venerable *Kelley Blue Book*
that list rough values for pretty much every motorcycle available, but the prices are a lot more volatile for
used motorcycles than they are for used cars. To make
matters more confusing, prices can vary wildly from
region to region. For example, a high-performance
sport bike will have more value in a metro area or
a rural area that has a lot of winding roads than it
will in a place with few metro areas and nothing but
flat, straight roads, places like North Dakota and
Kansas.

Regardless of the region, few people are getting
the kind of money that *KBB* lists for any motorcycle
since the economy imploded a few years back. Still,
you can use *KBB* prices as a jumping-off point. Remember to deduct the costs of any likely repairs or
needed maintenance from the prices listed in sources
like *KBB*.

A more accurate way to assess the current market
for a bike is to go on eBay and find as many examples
of the particular bike as you can. Even if you don't
plan to buy a bike on eBay, sign up for an eBay account and monitor the sales of the bikes you are interested in buying using the "My eBay" feature. After
spending a couple of weeks watching which bikes sell
and how much they sell for, you'll have a pretty fair
idea of the current market value of any used bike you
may want to buy.

If you're like most people, you'll try to negotiate the best deal possible, but like everyone else you meet, you should treat the seller with respect. This should be true whether you're buying from a private seller or a dealership. You can make a low-ball offer if you want, but if the offer is insultingly low, you better use a little humor when making it to avoid coming across as a crook. A salesperson at a dealership will just laugh off your offer by saying something like, "But seriously . . ." Your chances might not be much better with a private seller, but who knows? Maybe the seller will be desperate or inexperienced enough (or both) to take the offer.

In general, you have little to gain by nickel-and-diming the seller. If you've determined that a used bike is worthy of buying, saving a few hundred dollars on the purchase price won't mean much in the long run. If you like the bike and enjoy riding it, you'll have forgotten about the extra money just about as soon as you hit the open road.

FINANCING A BIKE

SPEAKING OF MONEY, BEFORE you even start looking at used bikes from private sellers, you have to make sure you have the capital to buy the bike or else you're wasting everyone's time. Ideally you should pay cash for everything you buy—paying interest on a loan is a huge waste of money—but the reality is that most people don't have enough spare cash sitting around to buy a motorcycle.

If you have to finance your bike, you at least should be smart about it. The interest paid in finance charges can represent a good chunk of the overall money you'll ultimately pay for the bike, so you should arrange for the lowest interest rate you can find.

First talk to the loan officer at your own bank. (If you have a decent credit rating, you will have at least one bank with which you regularly do business. If you don't have a bank, your credit rating will be poor and you'll be at the mercy of whatever loan shark is willing to lend you the money to buy a motorcycle.) See what interest rates and monthly payments will be for loans spread out over different time periods. Usually loans are paid off over a period of time ranging from thirty-six to seventy-two months. The longer the loan period, the lower the monthly payments, but the interest rate usually goes up as the time it takes to repay a loan gets longer.

After you've determined the best rate you can get from your bank, call at least two other banks to see if they can beat your bank's rate. This way you'll find the best rate available, but don't expect a good rate. You'll probably be in for a shock when you hear the rates for financing motorcycles, which are almost always much higher than the rates for financing cars. The rates you end up paying will vary from company to company, state to state, and person to person, and will depend on variables such as the prime rate and the borrower's credit rating. If you can't afford to pay cash, your best bet is to try to get a special financing deal from a factory, but those can be few and far between in times of tight credit. In general, if you buy a bike, especially a used bike, expect to pay close to double the interest rate you would get if you financed a new car. If you are financing a new bike from a dealership, you may be able to take advantage of special rates from the factory; but if you're financing a used bike, you'll just need to prepare to pay high interest rates.

In some cases those rates can approach the rates offered by your typical loan shark. Back when Harley sold more bikes than it built and had people paying $500 or more just to get on the waiting list to buy one of its motorcycles, the company's financial arm could charge whatever it wanted for interest. At one point the rate was as high as 21 percent. Just like the days of waiting lists to buy Harleys, the days of the Motor Company being able to charge outrageous interest rates are long gone now.

MOTORCYCLE INSURANCE

THE COST OF INSURING a motorcycle can rival the cost of maintaining and repairing it. This is especially true of high-performance sport bikes, which are grossly overrepresented in accident claims. That doesn't necessarily mean they're more prone to accidents, though you'd think that would be the case, judging from young people we've all seen riding their crotch rockets like lunatics. But in reality, middle-aged men aboard cruisers and touring bikes statistically account for more fatalities than do young squids on sport bikes. ("Squid" is a derogatory term for young people who ride recklessly aboard crotch rockets. No one knows exactly where the term came from. One theory is that it's because when they crash, they leave a squidlike blood splatter on the pavement.)

Though sport bikes don't account for the majority of accidents, they are justly overrepresented in insurance claims. This is because they are covered top to bottom in expensive plastic bodywork that lacks the protective features of most touring bikes like my Vision. If my bike falls over, or if a Honda Gold Wing or ST1300 falls over while standing still or at extremely low speeds, the bike's built-in design features prevent much serious damage from occurring. If a sport bike like a Honda CBR1000RR, Yamaha R1, or Suzuki GSX-R falls over, even while standing still in a parking lot, there will be thousands of dollars worth of broken plastic on the pavement.

Most owners simply can't absorb the cost of fixing that and have to rely on insurance payments to pay for the repair of their bikes. Often they won't have a choice but to repair the bikes since so many of them are financed by banks, and banks will require the owner to obtain full-coverage insurance. This brings up another advantage of paying cash for a bike rather than financing it; if you pay cash for a bike, you can save money by just obtaining liability insurance. (Most states will require you to at least have liability insurance.) If you finance a bike, you will have to obtain full-coverage insurance, which is much more expensive.

That said, even if you can get by with just liability insurance, it might be a good idea to get full coverage to protect your investment if your bike is worth a significant amount of money. If the cost is too high, you can save some money by going with a policy with a higher deductible. If you go with a $1,000 deductible (the amount you pay up front before insurance kicks in) instead of a $300 deductible, you'll have to cover more of the cost of any repairs for damage caused in an accident out of your own pocket, but at least you'll be able to recoup the bulk of the cost of your bike if it's totaled.

Besides, the higher deductibles you would pay in the event of an accident might not cost you that much more than having the insurance pay for the repair, because if you ever do file a motorcycle claim, most insurance companies will jack your rates up so much that it will more than equal the cost of any small repairs in the long run. Unless your bike has major damage, it can often cost you less to repair it without help from the insurance company once you figure in higher insurance premiums.

If you finance a bike, you may have the option of obtaining what is called "gap" insurance. This will pay the difference between what an insurance company pays for the value of a bike should you total it out and the amount that you may owe.

Chances are if you finance a new bike, you'll be upside down on your loan for most of the term of the loan because new motorcycles depreciate so quickly in value. (Being upside down on a loan means that you owe more on the loan than the item you financed is worth.) This means that if you wreck the bike or if it gets stolen, you won't collect enough on the insurance to cover the loan, so in addition to losing your motorcycle, you'll have to cough up a bunch of money to pay the difference. Gap insurance will pay that difference. If you have to finance your bike, the bank or dealer's financial department will likely offer you gap insurance. It might be a good idea to take them up on that offer.

Expect to be shocked when you find out how much you'll pay every month for full-coverage motorcycle insurance. If you have any moving violations or accident claims on your record, you may have difficulty finding insurance at any price. If you have automobile insurance with a company that also offers motorcycle insurance, going with the same company will likely be your least expensive option. You may even get a multivehicle discount. Unfortunately the odds are good that your auto insurer won't even offer motorcycle insurance. Because of high claim rates (remember, motorcycles fall over a lot more often than do automobiles), a lot of companies don't even offer motorcycle insurance.

Rates will vary from company to company, but there are some guidelines you can use when seeking insurance. Sport bikes or sport-tourers with a lot of plastic bodywork will be more expensive to insure than touring bikes for the reasons described previously. In general, bigger bikes will be more expensive to insure than smaller bikes, at least within the same category. A big cruiser may be cheaper to insure than a small sport bike, but it will be more expensive than a smaller cruiser. And a small sport bike will cost more than a large touring bike, but it will cost less than insuring a big sport bike.

Where you live will also affect your insurance rates. Companies base their rates on crash and theft

statistics in a given region. If you live in a neighborhood where a lot of motorcycle thefts have been re-
ported, you will have higher insurance rates than if
you lived in a suburb with low rates of motor vehicle
theft. Sometimes the statistics are surprising—some
so-called nice neighborhoods have high theft rates—
but, in general, the farther you live from an inner
city, the lower your insurance rates will be. If you
live in a rural area, you'll most likely have the lowest
rates of all.

BUYING A NEW MOTORCYCLE

BUYING A NEW BIKE is in most ways much simpler
than purchasing a used machine. You won't need to
examine every component of a new bike because it
won't have any wear and tear to examine. Likewise
you won't need to look for evidence of abuse and improper maintenance, since you'll be first person to
use (or abuse) and maintain the bike.

Even though you'll spend more buying a new
bike, there are some good reasons to go this route if
you can afford it. You can never be sure that a used
bike was properly cared for, regardless how thoroughly you inspect it. You'll be the person who controls how well maintained a new bike will be.

When you're shopping for a used bike, you'll
look for the best available bike that suits your needs.
When shopping for a new bike, you'll have your pick
of any bike that falls into the price range you establish
for yourself. Deciding which ones you want to look

at is the fun part, because your research will consist of reading about each bike in motorcycle magazines and on motorcycle websites.

BEWARE OF "BETA TESTING" NEW BIKES

ONE WORD OF ADVICE when picking out a new bike— be cautious when buying a newly introduced model. Sometimes manufacturers have an unwritten policy of beta testing; that is, the first few examples of a new bike might not have had all the bugs worked out of them in the development process, making the buyers an unwitting part of that process. Because of the pressure to meet production schedules, manufacturers sometimes push new models out the door before they're completely ready and then they work out any potential problems on the fly.

Harley-Davidson is considered the worst offender in this respect. Longtime riders will tell you never to buy a first-year version of any Harley. This has probably been true since Harley and the Davidson brothers cobbled together their first prototype bike in 1903, but it has definitely been true since at least the introduction of the Knucklehead in 1936.

In 1936 recirculating oil systems were still relatively new. Instead of high-pressure pumps that circulated oil through the engine, earlier total-loss engines just had a hand pump that a rider would pump every so often to lubricate the engine. This oil would circulate around the engine and then either be burned or slosh out through one of the many areas on the engine where moving parts were exposed, most commonly through the valve train. Recirculating oiling systems were a huge step forward in engine reliability, but designers of early examples like Harley's 1936 Knucklehead didn't fully comprehend the need to contain the oil being circulated by the high-pressure oil pump, so they didn't fully enclose the valve gear. As a result, the very first Knuckleheads sprayed their riders with hot oil from the valve train. Harley quickly remedied this by designing tin cups that snapped over the exposed valve gear, but the problem wasn't really solved until Motor Company engineers redesigned the valve train so that it was completely enclosed.

This sort of problem-solving-on-the-fly approach has been a pattern with Harley ever since. The early Panheads had major problems with their hydraulic lifters, problems that weren't solved until the lifters were moved from the tops of the pushrods down into the crankcases. The first electric-start Electra Glides also suffered teething problems, as did the newly introduced Shovelheads, alternator-equipped Shovelheads, and the first bikes equipped with five-speed transmissions.

The first-year Evolution engines had so many problems that for years a lot of riders wore T-shirts that read: SEE NO EVO. HEAR NO EVO. SPEAK NO EVO. When the Evolution was later replaced with the Twin Cam 88, a mechanic friend of mine hurried up and bought one of the last Evolution-powered bikes because he knew the new TC88 engines would have problems. He was right. The TC88 engine came out in 1999. At the Sturgis rally in 2000 the sides of South Dakota roads were littered with TC88 engines that had suffered catastrophic failure of their camshaft bearings.

Harley eventually worked out the bugs in all of these engines, but the pattern continues to this day. Even though the 96-cubic-inch Twin Cam engine was just an enlarged version of the TC88, early examples of that engine suffered from overheating problems. You should flat out avoid buying the first-year (and often even the second-year) examples of any new product from Harley-Davidson.

Just because Harley is the worst offender doesn't mean other companies don't follow the same practice. Even competent non-Italian manufacturers can be guilty of beta testing every now and then. Usually, new bikes from Germany and Japan are good to go from the first day of production, but every now and then a motorcycle slips out of every factory before all the bugs are worked out.

FINDING A GOOD MOTORCYCLE SHOP

ONCE YOU'VE DETERMINED WHICH bikes you want to look at, you'll need to find dealerships that sell those brands. Just finding dealerships used to be tough since up until a few years ago most motorcycle shops were little out-of-the-way holes in the ground. Historically motorcycle sales didn't generate the kind of cash flow that allowed dealers to open up high-profile shops in good retail locations.

But that changed in the late 1990s and early 2000s, thanks in large part to the success of Harley-Davidson. A company that was almost bankrupt in early 1986, Harley-Davidson's fortunes dramatically changed in the late 1980s. The Motor Company's rags-to-riches story became the stuff of legend, and by the early 1990s Harley was one of the most successful companies in America.

In large part Harley's success was as much the result of its marketing clothing and accessories as it was the result of its motorcycle sales. And the company wasn't just selling exhaust pipes and T-shirts; by the early 1990s Harley shops sold just about any product you could imagine emblazoned with the company's famous bar-and-shield logo, from toilet-seat covers to cigarettes.

Because retailing products other than motorcycles was such a big part of its business model, Harley forced its dealers to build new facilities on prime commercial real estate. These new Harley superstores were more like expensive boutique shops than the traditional motorcycle dealerships that used to be found on the wrong side of the tracks, sandwiched between a scrap-iron yard and a whorehouse.

By the early 1990s Harley dominated the American motorcycle market; where Harley led, the other manufacturers followed. By the mid-2000s just about every motorcycle dealership had moved from its previous steel sheds hidden in industrial parks into big, fancy showrooms in high-buck retail areas. It used to be that you'd need a phone book and a good map to find a motorcycle shop in a strange city; today you can hardly miss them because they're right along the freeway, next to the Audi dealerships and Cracker Barrel restaurants.

Although you won't have to track down motorcycle shops like we did in the old days, you will have to do a little research to see which shops are good and which should be avoided, because not all motorcycle shops are created equal. Each one is staffed by human beings, and the excellence of a shop is only as good as the quality of those individuals.

To determine the quality of the staff will require two things of you. The first is that you have some knowledge of the bike you're looking at, which you will have, since you followed my advice and did some research. Second, you have to use your knowledge of human nature. You need to have a feel for whether someone is telling you the truth or feeding you a line of bullshit. Developing that sort of intuition is beyond the scope of this book.

THE SERVICE DEPARTMENT

A CRITICAL FACTOR IN finding the right dealership is the quality of a shop's service department. It really doesn't matter how straight a shooter a salesperson might be if the service department is staffed by morons.

For example, when I first saw Harley's then-new V-Rod, I was visiting a Harley shop while traveling out of state. I wasn't interested in buying the bike, but I was curious about its maintenance costs. I knew

Porsche had designed the overhead-cam engine, and Porsche has a reputation for building engines that are idiotically expensive to maintain. I'd stopped at the Harley shop to get a part for my Road King and decided to ask the service manager how much it cost to do a major service on the V-Rod.

The guy told me that it would be the same as the cost of the major service of any other V-twin. To comprehend the sheer stupidity this man exhibited, you need to understand something about Harley's air-cooled V-twins and the V-Rod engine. The air-cooled V-twin, the engine that's found in every Harley except the various V-Rod models, uses the same basic overhead valve system the company has used since the 1936 Knucklehead, which has the cam (or cams) located down in the case moving pushrods that go up to the top end and open the valves. These pushrods have featured hydraulic lifters since before I started riding, which means that the valves never need to be adjusted.

The V-Rod uses overhead cams that don't have hydraulic lifters, meaning that like most high-performance motorcycles they need periodic valve adjustments. The valve adjustment is usually the most expensive part of a major tune-up. When the service manager said the cost for a V-Rod tune-up was the same as the tune-up for any other V-twin, I asked him if that meant they adjusted the valves on the V-Rod for free.

I don't know if I've ever seen a man look so befuddled. Here was a man so ignorant about motorcycle mechanics that he didn't even know he had to adjust the valves on Harley's new V-Rod (which, it turns out, is a ridiculously expensive process because the engine has to be dropped to gain access to the rear valves). And this fool was the shop's service manager. I wouldn't want anyone this ignorant checking the air pressure in my tires, much less supervising the people who might be rebuilding my engine.

I asked around, and it turns out that I'm not the only person who wasn't impressed with this shop and its service department. A lot of the local riders I spoke with refused to do business with the shop; instead, many of them drove an extra seventy miles to do business with a respected shop in a neighboring state.

If it's possible to meet with local motorcyclists, you can get a good idea from talking to them which shops are good and which should be avoided. You can also learn a bit about this by snooping around online and trying to find local motorcycle forums, but remember, like anything else you read on the Internet, take what you read with a grain of salt. Sometimes customers are to blame, but that doesn't stop them from unfairly lambasting a dealership on the Internet.

Ultimately you have to make the decision as to where you're going to shop for a bike. Again, you need to have a pretty good knowledge of motorcycles to accurately gauge the competency of a shop and its service department. If you don't feel comfortable with your own knowledge base, try to enlist the help of a friend who knows something about motorcycles.

FINAL NEGOTIATIONS

ONCE YOU'VE FOUND THE bike of your dreams from an independent seller or the right shop, one with a competent sales staff and a good service department, it's time to negotiate a price. You'll have less room to negotiate the price of a new bike than you will a used bike. As mentioned in the last chapter, dealerships have to make some money on each bike they sell just to keep their doors open. That said, there's no reason why you have to foot the entire bill for their overhead. There has to be a little compromise on the parts of both you and the dealer.

Most dealers will do what they can to meet you halfway, but in recent decades that has not been the case with Harley dealers. For many years, selling Harleys consisted of sitting behind a desk, collecting $500 deposits, and putting names on a list. The dealers had little incentive to compromise with a buyer. Today the motorcycle market is very different, and Harley sales are down dramatically. Harley dealers have been slow to change their stubborn ways, but they will have to adapt to survive. Those dealers that are unwilling to compromise will become extinct.

Typically dealers add a base margin of 12 to 18 percent on new bikes. They often add extra charges on top of that, like freight and setup costs. They also make money from their finance department by talking you into things like extended warranties.

Your best tool for finding a dealership with the

lowest markup is still the old-fashioned telephone. You can find a lot of dealerships advertising on the Internet, but they usually aren't listing the lowest prices they have available. More often they seem to be fishing for buyers willing to pay a bit more. For example, a shop might list a bike at $11,000 on its webpage but if you call and talk to a salesperson, you might find that you can get a one- or two-year-old carry-over version of the exact same bike for $8,000.

Make certain you ask for an out-the-door price when shopping via phone. Make it clear that you want the salesperson to include all extra charges like freight and setup costs as well as the costs of license plates and sales tax. This way you're comparing apples to apples when talking to salespeople from different dealerships; it also ensures you won't be surprised by additional costs when you go to buy the bike.

If you can't get a straight answer from a salesperson, you're best off avoiding that dealership. If the person says something like "Come on down and we'll talk about it," he or she is trying to lure you into that dealership. There are plenty of motorcycle shops out there; you don't need to deal with one that tries to trick you right from the start.

You'll be able to get somewhat of an idea about what dealers are paying for the wholesale price of a bike from the range of prices you find when calling around. You can figure that the lowest prices are marked up around 12 percent from the wholesale cost and the highest prices are marked up around 18 percent. Do the math and you'll have a rough idea of what the wholesale cost is.

You can negotiate from there, but chances are you'll have a hard time getting the price down much below the lowest price you find when shopping around. What you can do is use this information to negotiate the best price at the best dealership you found while researching dealerships. If the best price is available at a dealership with a lousy service department or a bad reputation, you can try to negotiate the same price from a dealership with a decent service department and a better reputation.

PULLING THE TRIGGER

IF YOU'RE BUYING FROM a dealership in your own state, the dealership will take care of getting license plates for a bike and paying the sales tax. It will roll that cost into your out-the-door price. But if you're buying from an out-of-state dealership or a private party, you'll need to take care of tax and licensing yourself.

There are some ways to make this process simpler and safer. For example, it's a good idea to write up some sort of simple contract between you and the seller. This doesn't have to be a formal document drawn up by a lawyer. It just needs to be a document written in plain, easily understandable language that outlines the terms to which you and the buyer agree. Both you and the seller should have a signed copy of the agreement.

Before any money changes hands, you'll need to make sure you have all the paperwork you'll need when you go to your state department of motor vehicles for your license plates. You'll need a clear title, and you'll need to make sure that the VIN (vehicle identification number) and engine numbers are correct and match the title. If there's some discrepancy, you may find it impossible to get a license plate for your bike.

WHAT YOU SHOULD KNOW

- Be prepared before going to buy a motorcycle—have your financing and insurance in order before you even go to look at a bike.
- Avoid financing if you can help it because it makes buying a motorcycle much more expensive.
- Make sure you can afford to insure a motorcycle before you buy it.

CHAPTER SIX

ADVANCED RIDING TECHNIQUES

Now that you've learned enough about motorcycles to decide what type you want, you've learned how to ride, and you've bought a motorcycle, I'm going to talk about the most important thing you can do while riding a motorcycle: staying alive. In this chapter we're going to discuss advanced training and riding techniques, including cornering, braking, and coping with other vehicles.

More than anything else in this book, the information that follows will help keep you alive. But as with the information in chapter 3, your best bet is still to get professional training. Once again, the Motorcycle Safety Foundation is a good place to start when looking for advanced training: in the late 1980s MSF developed its Experienced RiderCourse (ERC), a half-day course for newer riders and seasoned riders alike that's designed to hone bikers' riding skills as well as help develop the mental skills that will keep people alive out on the meat-grinding public highways. I took the ERC back when it first came out in the 1980s. I'd sent so many new riders to the basic RiderCourse that I thought I should take a course myself. I had nearly thirty years of experience when I took the ERC, and I still found it extremely helpful (even though I was the only rider in the entire class who fell down).

If you want to take your riding skills to the next level, you might want to consider going to one of the many high-performance riding schools available. These usually are held at racetracks and use motorcycles provided by the school, though some, like Lee Parks's Total Control Advanced Riding Clinic, take place in large parking lots and require you to provide your own motorcycle. (See the appendix for more information about riding courses.)

The fact that you're reading this book bodes well for your future survival as a motorcyclist. I'm trying to share a lifetime of experience with you, and I hope you'll find it useful, but I can't stress strongly enough the need to get proper training. Ideally you'll use the information in this section of the book in conjunction with what you learn in an advanced riding course.

SITUATIONAL AWARENESS

AWARENESS OF YOUR SURROUNDINGS will usually be the critical factor that determines whether you live or die out on public roads. You need to be aware of what you are doing at all times, you need to be aware of what other people are doing, and you need to make other drivers aware of what you are doing.

Being aware of your own actions is the element over which you have the most control. An obvious way of doing that is to ride sober. Normally I don't care what people do. I figure it's their business. If they want to have a beer or three, I don't see a problem with that. Likewise I don't really care if they like to burn a marijuana cigarette now and then. Hell, I don't really care if they're drunk and high all the time, if they snort Drano or bang rat poison. It's their business, and it really doesn't matter whether or not I approve. Abuse yourself in whatever way you see fit, but when it comes time to ride a motorcycle, I highly recommend riding sober.

The Hurt Report found that alcohol was involved in nearly half of all motorcycle fatalities. That was thirty years ago, but the number has remained relatively stable. In 1998, 45 percent of motorcycle fatalities involved alcohol; in 2004, 48 percent involved alcohol. The problem is that alcohol and other drugs slow down your reaction time, and reaction time is everything when it comes to crashing or not crashing your motorcycle. When something happens—when that deer jumps out in front of you or that car swerves into your lane because the driver didn't see you—you have only a fraction of a second to react. If your reactions are an instant too slow because you have had even one beer, that could easily mean the difference between life and death.

Last year on the way home from Sturgis a couple

of deer—a doe and a fawn—ran out in front of me. I was able to slow down just enough to miss the mother as she ran across the road, but not the fawn. Luckily for both of us the fawn didn't cross the road, but instead, ran alongside me before turning back into the forest. I was stone-cold sober and paying attention, and even then, I barely reacted fast enough to avoid hitting the larger deer. Had I drank even one beer, that might have slowed my reaction time just enough to cause me to hit the deer.

But other distractions can impair your reaction times almost as much as alcohol and other drugs. The main cause of distracted driving these days is the cell phone. If you're calling on your cell phone or, worse yet, texting while you're riding your motorcycle, well, you deserve to be killed, preferably sooner rather than later. That's all I have to say about that subject.

Still other distractions exist that are less obvious because they're inside your own head. When you ride, are you focusing on what you're doing and the potential hazards that are all around you, or are you thinking about giving your boss that beat down he's deserved for all these years? Are you thinking about the condition of your motorcycle, or are you thinking about the condition of your marriage? If you're concentrating on the fight you just had with your wife when you told her you were going for a motorcycle ride, you're probably not concentrating on that cell-phone-yakking half-wit in the SUV that's barreling down on you.

I lost a good friend this way. The guy was a skilled rider and extremely safety conscious—he was one of the first people I ever knew who wore a helmet. His motorcycle was always in tip-top condition, and he never rode when he was drunk or high. But one day he got in an argument with his girlfriend, took off on his bike, lost control in a corner, and hit an oak tree.

It's impossible to clear your mind of all distractions all the time—if we could, the makers of sleeping pills, Prozac, and other mental medications would be out of business—but before you head out on the road, you have to do everything you can to empty your mind of anything that will disrupt your focus on riding. Do whatever it takes to clear your head, including going to the bathroom. (You'd be surprised how much your concentration can suffer when you've got a full bladder.)

Anger is another huge distraction, but it's hard not to get angry when you're sharing the road with the collection of simpletons known as other drivers. Anger clouds your judgment and slows your reaction time. You'll often have every reason in the world to be angry at other drivers, but you need to remain calm, cool, and collected in every situation, regardless of who is right and who is wrong. Above all, don't get into road-rage situations with other vehicles. They may be completely wrong, but they have your life in their hands. Right or wrong, you can't win an argument with someone who has the ability to end your life by simply turning his or her steering wheel.

Buddhist monks spend entire lifetimes trying to figure out how to clear these sorts of distractions from their minds. Maybe it works for them; maybe it doesn't. I don't know—I've spent my life doing other things. Like riding motorcycles. Since I don't expect to become a Buddhist monk anytime soon, I've had to find other ways to clear my mind when I'm on my bike.

One trick I've developed is to focus my attention on potential hazards. I study my surroundings and imagine what might go wrong. I look for brush or other growth along the road that might block my view of a deer or other critter that might run out in front of me. I watch other traffic, looking for other vehicles that might swerve into my lane, or trucks with loads that might come loose or tires that might blow out, sending debris onto the road.

I look for any element that might pose danger, then I check to see how prepared I am to deal with that danger. Have I placed my motorcycle in the best position to deal with potential hazards? Do I have enough room to maneuver out of the way of danger? (I'll talk more about lane positioning later.) Am I covering my front brake with my right fingers so that I don't lose a fraction of a second reaching for my brake if the situation goes south in a hurry? Is my engine in its powerband so that if I need to accelerate out of the way of danger, I won't twist my throttle only to have the engine bog down? Am I traveling at a safe speed in the first place?

In addition to assessing how prepared I am to deal with potential dangers, I devise plans of action in case something does go wrong. I look at the way a load on a truck is tied down to try to determine which way the debris is likely to fall if the ties come loose, then look for a clear, safe space to move in the opposite direction of where the debris will likely fall. I try to determine possible paths of travel of even the most errant vehicle. I allow plenty of room between me and the vehicle in front of me, and I position my bike so that I have the best view of any potential danger. If I spot potential danger, I reposition my bike so that I have the least exposure to that threat and the best possible escape routes if the worst-case scenario comes to pass.

This exercise helps me prepare for potential danger, but it does more than that: it focuses my complete attention on that moment in time, so that I'm not thinking about anything other than riding my motorcycle in that place in time. It might not be the same as spending a lifetime in some Buddhist monastery, but the concentration required while riding a motorcycle is a form of focused meditation that makes all the petty distractions of day-to-day life melt away. It might seem morbid to concentrate on potential danger with such intense focus, but it clears my head. When I'm finished riding, I feel relaxed and recharged, so morbid or not, I consider it a beneficial activity. Some people ride with stereos blasting at top volume, but to me that would interrupt my meditation on the ride. The only sound track I need for that is the music my engine makes when it's running in peak condition.

DEFEATING ROAD HAZARDS

THINK OF GOING OUT on public roads aboard a motorcycle as a form of going to war. As in any form of combat, the only way to win is to know your enemy. You can better understand the nature of the threats you'll face if you break down the types of hazards into three broad categories:

- **Vehicles.** These include everything from a fast-moving bicycle to a double-trailer semitruck. This category has the most potential to kill a motorcycle rider, so you should never trust any other vehicle. Obviously the bigger the vehicle, the more potential harm it can do to you; but when you're on a bike, you are so vulnerable that even an errant bicycle rider can potentially take you out. Learn to identify the vehicles that are most likely to kill you, and when you're riding among them, always look for possible escape routes should things start to go wrong.

- **Debris and potholes.** This category includes any stationary object that can lead to your losing control of your motorcycle if you hit it. This could be the road alligators from one of the thousands of blown truck tires that you'll be dodging as long as you ride motorcycles, or it could be a sign post at the edge of the road, or a box of bolts that fell off a flatbed truck. You'll need to perfect your control over your motorcycle to develop the riding skills that will help you avoid hitting this type of hazard.

- **People and other animals.** People and other animals move slower than vehicles, but they can be almost as deadly—and even more erratic. They can change direction quickly, and they don't follow normal patterns of movement, as vehicular traffic does. When you're moving down the road on your motorcycle, you'll often ride in conditions that make it difficult to see animals and pedestrians until they pop out right in front of you, so you'll need to learn to recognize the situations in which two- or four-legged critters are likely to appear.

When riding on public highways, I recommend adopting the attitude that every single person on the road is a sociopathic serial killer who has just escaped from an asylum for the criminally insane. This might seem a little pessimistic, but you'll live longer if you assume everyone else on the road is a homicidal moron whose sole purpose is to kill you.

Face it: an unsettlingly high percentage of American drivers are unfit to be behind the wheel in the best of circumstances. What else would you expect in a country where the hardest part of the driving test is parallel parking? Parking is the opposite of driving, so there's not a hell of a lot of actual driving involved in getting a driver's license. Technically it should be called a parking license, but it's not, and the end result is a nation of people who think of the driver's seat as a place to make phone calls and send text messages while they are going somewhere else. There's not much you can depend on anymore, but you can be virtually certain that someone is going to do something incredibly stupid out on the road. The best way to deal with the situation is to make certain that person is not you.

You need to have complete awareness of every single one of the idiots with whom you're sharing the road while you are out on your bike. You need to learn to read traffic and learn to recognize the clues that will alert you to potentially dangerous situations. You need to develop a feel for the circumstances in which other drivers are likely to do something stupid.

For example, when you are on a multilane road, pulling up to an intersection alongside a line of cars, you can be sure that at least one of them is going to pull out into your lane to get around that line, and you can be just as sure that the person will not have checked his or her mirror or looked over his or her shoulder to clear the lane, so he or she has no idea you are there. Or when you're riding along a row of parked cars, expect at least one of them to pull out in front of you or even beside you.

When you're riding alongside slow-moving or parked traffic, always position your bike as far away from the line of cars as possible to give yourself room to react when the car inevitably pulls out right in front of you. Constantly scan for safe space in which you can swerve around the damned fool. Monitor your rearview mirror to make certain no one will run you over if the only safe course of action is to brake hard. Create circumstances in which you have the most possible options in the event of any dangerous situation.

Don't ever believe anyone's turn signals. The person may be driving down the road totally oblivious to the fact that his or her turn signal is flashing. If he or she does plan to change lanes, he or she is more likely to not use the signals at all. The person changing lanes without signaling a lane change will probably be the life-threatening situation you encounter most often. It will happen with such frequency that you'll soon be surprised when someone does signal a lane change and doesn't pull into your lane while you are occupying it.

To prevent this you need to be completely aware of what everyone on the road is doing at all times. The best way to determine if a person is about to change lanes isn't to watch his or her turn signal; it's to watch his or her front tires. Before a car can change direction, its front tires have to turn. Where the front tires turn, the car will follow. If you see the tires turn toward your spot on the road, you have an extra split second to react, find a safe space, and move out of harm's way.

Watching the front tires of cars is especially useful for alerting you when oncoming cars are about to make a left turn across your lane. This is an exceptionally dangerous situation. Unfortunately it's also a common occurrence—I've been almost taken out by oncoming cars making unsignaled left turns in front of me more than all other near misses combined. To be fair to other drivers, motorcycles are hard to see in the best conditions; when they are coming right at you, they don't present a very large profile and are even easier to miss. Factor in the 50 percent chance that the oncoming driver is distracted because his main squeeze is "sexting" him, and for all practical purposes you're invisible.

Because of this you'll likely have someone making a turn across your lane of traffic on a weekly basis. Sometimes it will be on a daily basis. And it won't always happen at obvious intersections. Often the person will be turning into a driveway or a parking lot that you might not have seen. The other driver may even be making a U-turn. I lost a friend in December

2009 because a van made an unsignaled U-turn and pulled out just as he was passing by. And this man was as experienced a rider as I've ever known.

You can't prevent this situation, but you can prepare for it, and, as I've mentioned, one of the best ways to do that is to watch the front tires of other vehicles. If a car is coming at you, watch its left front tire. Position yourself so that you're as far away from the vehicle as possible, and ride in a place that will leave you room to get out of the way should you see the other vehicle's left wheel start to turn in your direction.

Watching the front tires of other vehicles won't make you invincible, but it will give you extra time to react to danger. If you are paying attention and notice the instant someone turns a front tire toward your lane, you'll have an extra fraction of a second to react, and that fraction of a second could save your life. But this only helps if you're aware of your surroundings. To be effective, your reaction will have to take into account every other numb-nuts driver on the road. You won't be gaining much if you swerve to miss a car moving into your lane from the right and accidentally hit the car in the lane to your left.

You'll also have to be aware of all the nonvehicular hazards. For example, when you're riding along a line of parked cars, it's just as likely that a dog or a child will run out from between the parked cars as it is that one of the parked cars will pull out in front of you. There's no way to predict the behavior of an animal or a child; the best you can do is try to identify places where an animal or a child might possibly emerge onto a road. Be aware of your surroundings, cover your front brake lever, and be prepared to make an emergency stop the instant you see something moving into your path of travel.

Sometimes the nonmoving hazards can be as deadly as the moving ones. You need to be aware of road conditions that could lead to a loss of traction, like rain, dirt, leaves, railroad tracks, potholes, oil, antifreeze, ice, and sand or gravel buildup. Debris is especially dangerous when you encounter it in a curve. It tends to build up on the outside edge of a curve, so you need to give this area extra attention when you are scanning the road in a corner.

If there is debris in a corner, slow down to give yourself time to maneuver around it. If it takes you by surprise and there isn't enough time to avoid it, don't panic and hit the brakes. This will upset your chassis and increase the chances that you'll lose traction and crash. Instead, maintain a steady speed through the corner. If you've slowed down to a safe speed before entering the corner, you should be all right. If you are going too fast and need to slow down in a corner, stand the bike up for a brief moment, brake, then immediately countersteer back into the corner. If you react quickly, you should be able to maintain control of your motorcycle, but if you stand the bike up and brake for more than a split second, there's a good chance you'll run off the road.

Even the paint on the road itself can be hazardous. The paint of the center stripe and at the edge of the road, or in a crosswalk, or warning of an approaching railroad crossing, or words such as STOP AHEAD can get as slippery as mud or ice, especially when wet. If you have Speed Channel, watch a mo-

torcycle road race in the rain some time. You'll see
that even the best riders in the world will crash the
instant their tire hits some wet paint on the surface
of the racetrack.

The paint doesn't even have to be wet to be dangerous. Sometimes when the temperature gets high
enough, the paint starts to melt and turn into a sub-
stance that resembles slippery wet vinyl. When your
tire hits this, your whole bike can slide to one side or
the other. If you're not prepared or overreact, you can
find yourself doing a face plant into the pavement.
Always treat paint on pavement as a low-traction
surface, especially when the weather has been wet or
extremely hot.

MAKING YOURSELF VISIBLE

IN ADDITION TO BEING aware of your surroundings
and the other drivers, you need to make other drivers
aware of you. When another driver says he didn't see
the motorcyclist he just killed, he's most likely telling
the truth. Motorcycles are small vehicles compared
with all the four-wheeled traffic on the road, and it's
easy for other drivers to miss seeing them.

Your job is to make that less easy. It helps to wear
bright-colored clothing and helmets, or even wear
vests and riding suits made of reflective high-visibility
material. You might even want to consider getting
a brightly colored motorcycle. I find that when I'm
riding a brightly colored bike, say yellow or orange,
I have a lot fewer situations where people make left

turns in front of me than I do when I'm riding a black bike.

But I'm somewhat limited in what I can wear when it comes to reflective vests. I'm a member of a club, and one of the club's bylaws is that I have to wear a garment prominently displaying that club's insignia when I ride. Plus I like black motorcycles, so I start out with two strikes against me. Even so, there's a lot I can do to make myself more visible when I'm riding, like riding with my high beam on during the day. This goes a long way toward getting the attention of other drivers.

I also make a point of always signaling my lane changes and turns early, giving other drivers time to notice my bike and see what I'm going to do next. When I change lanes, for example, once I've looked in my mirrors and determined that the lane I'm moving into is clear, I activate my turn signals early and sometimes even supplement the turn signal with a hand signal, just so there is no question about my intentions. I get stopped by the cops all the time (I think they watch too much television and believe everything they see). Often the cops will say they stopped me because I didn't use my turn signal. When they say this, I know I'm dealing with a dishonest cop, because I *always* use my turn signal.

Another trick I've developed for making myself more visible is to give my brake pedal a light tap, even when I'm not slowing or stopping, just to make my brake light flash and get the attention of cars that may be behind me. And I'm not afraid to use my horn. I don't give a damn about being polite when it comes to life-or-death situations, and if another driver doesn't see me, my life is in danger. If it takes a blast from my horn to let the other driver know I'm there, then I'll blast my horn.

One thing to remember: even if you think you've got the attention of another driver, don't bet your life on it. The driver might be looking right at you—you may even think you've made eye contact with him or her—but in reality the person is looking right through you. Instead of seeing you, he or she could be looking at a cell-phone screen, reading a text message.

ZONES OF AWARENESS

To BE AWARE OF what's going on around you, scan your surroundings in a methodical way. Your eyes are your tools for getting information about what's going on around you. To get the most out of them, you need to keep them moving all the time. Don't let your eyes fixate on any one object for more than a fraction of a second. Once you've determined something isn't a threat, move on to the next thing.

Scan all aspects of your surroundings, and don't just focus on other traffic. Watch for animals, debris, and the condition of road surfaces. Keep your eyes open for piles of loose gravel or sand in corners, which can be as slippery as ice. Make sure you include your rearview mirror as part of the landscape you're scanning, but also turn your head slightly to check your blind spots, especially when turning, stopping, or changing lanes (again, see the upcoming information about soft lane changes).

You need to pay more attention to some areas than others on a motorcycle. Imagine the region around your bike is the face of a clock. Because you are always traveling forward on a motorcycle, the area between eleven o'clock and one o'clock is the area from which danger will come at you most rapidly and most frequently, so this area should get the lion's share of your time when scanning. Focus on your intended path. Concentrate on the area about twelve to fourteen seconds ahead of your bike, since you'll need at least this much time to react in an emergency situation. Keep your eyes up. This will aim your vision ahead, where the greatest danger lies.

Watch for subtle clues, like a shadow on the road ahead. It might indicate some oil, fresh tar, or some other slippery surface that could cause you to lose traction and crash. Be aware of movement in the bushes on the edge of the road, which could be a sign that an animal is about to enter the road in front of you.

You need to make the area in front of you your primary focus, but that doesn't mean you can ignore the other areas. You need to pay attention to what you see out of the corners of your eyes. A flash of movement might be a deer getting ready to jump out in front of you, or it might be a car pulling out of a driveway into your lane. Or that SUV barreling down on you in your rearview mirror might be driven by some texting fool who really doesn't see you. Most danger will come at you from the front, but you need to be aware of all 360 degrees of your surroundings, from twelve o'clock back to twelve o'clock, especially at intersections.

INTERSECTIONS

INTERSECTIONS ARE THE MOST dangerous places you can be on a motorcycle, because they are where other vehicles behave most unpredictably, but you can do a lot to minimize the danger. Remember, an intersection is anywhere that traffic can cross your lane of traffic. This means that driveways and other crossings are forms of intersections.

The most dangerous intersections are the odd ones where several roads converge at once. You'll encounter these where multiple roads meet or where frontage roads run along a main road. The average car driver always seems to be confused to some degree; at complicated intersections, the degree of confusion spikes and people drive in an especially stupid manner because they don't know what they are supposed to do.

Blind driveways and blind intersections have to run a close second to complicated intersections for degrees of danger, but they're all dangerous. Following a few simple practices can make them less dangerous:

- Slow down when riding through any intersection. The more dangerous the type of intersection, the more you should slow down. Slowing down puts you in control of the situation by giving you more time to scan the intersection for potential dangers. The earlier you can detect possible danger, the more time you have to prepare to deal with it.

- Make certain an intersection is clear before you proceed through it. Be sure that the person in a stopped car isn't just changing the CD in the stereo or applying makeup. If that is the case, the driver may finish doing whatever it is he or she is doing and pull into your lane just as you're passing through the intersection.

- When passing through an intersection, be extra diligent about practicing the other safety techniques discussed elsewhere in this book: cover your front brake lever, watch the front tires of other vehicles, and position your bike so that you have the best visibility and are most visible, and so that you have the most safe space in which to maneuver.

When passing through an intersection while another vehicle is blocking your view, pay extra attention to possible left-turning vehicles that you might not see at first. If the vehicle blocking your view is in the left lane and you're in the right lane, you can position yourself for the best view by riding on the far right side of your lane, positioning yourself as far away from potential left-turning vehicles as possible. If you're following the vehicle, your best position might be on the far left side of the lane, where you'll be most visible to the turning vehicle.

As you prepare to stop at an intersection, pay special attention to the vehicles behind you. Be even more careful if you're stopping on a yellow light because a lot of people interpret a yellow light as a signal to floor it and drive like hell. That person may be looking at the light, or at traffic in the cross street, and might not even see you until he or she has run you down.

This situation is so lethal that you should always scan for a possible escape route in case you need one. Choose the side of the road that will give you the most room to maneuver, which will usually be the side of the lane that is farthest away from oncoming traffic. When you do stop, don't pull right up behind the vehicle in front of you; that way, if someone behind you doesn't stop, the emergency escape route that you identified as you entered the intersection won't be blocked by the vehicle in front of you.

It's important to always leave yourself enough room to maneuver whenever you stop, whether you're at an intersection or not. Even when you have to stop because freeway traffic stops moving, monitor the traffic behind you. Make sure you have room to move forward, even if that means you have to ride between parked cars. That way if someone behind you doesn't stop, you'll have at least some sort of clear space to use for getting out of the vehicle's path.

To do this, your bike will have to be ready to go. When you sit at an intersection, or anytime you have to stop where there is traffic around you, make sure you leave your bike in first gear, with the clutch lever pulled in. That way if you need to get out of someone's way in a hurry, you won't lose any time shifting into gear. Remember, a split second is the difference between living and dying.

Leaving my bike in first gear has been a hard habit for me to adopt. When I started riding, motorcycles had foot-operated clutches and hand-operated shifters. The shifters would be operated with a lever attached to the gas tank that was connected to the transmission with linkage rods that ran down from the tank. These shifters never really worked well because of all that sloppy linkage, so we used to get rid of the linkage and use levers coming straight out of the transmission for shifting. We called them "suicide shifters."

Using a suicide shifter meant that we had to push in the clutch with our left foot and reach down and shift with our left hand. This was an awkward operation while moving, but when a bike was stopped, keeping the bike in gear while holding the clutch pedal down with one foot bordered on impossible. We had to shift into neutral before we stopped so that we could let the clutch pedal out and hold the stopped bike up with both feet. This habit became so strongly ingrained in me that to this day I have to remind myself to keep my bike in gear at a stop.

BLIND SPOTS

I SUSPECT THAT POORLY designed driver's education programs over the past sixty or seventy years are responsible for a lot of the lousy driving habits we have today. I know they are responsible for the fact that, by my count, seven out of eight drivers don't know how to use their side-view mirrors.

Side-view mirrors are a relatively recent tool in

the United States. Europeans had them for many years, but we didn't really start to get them on cars until the 1970s, and when we did get them, no one knew how to use them correctly. Especially driver's ed teachers. Side-view mirrors are designed to cover the blind spots you can't see with your rearview mirror, but for many years driver's ed teachers taught kids that they were supposed to point the mirrors at their rear bumpers. For all I know, they still do. When the side-view mirrors are pointed at the rear bumper, the driver sees only the same area in the side-view mirrors as he or she does in the rearview mirror, and his or her blind spot is still as blind as ever.

The correct way to use side-view mirrors is to position them so that you can see what's in the blind spots to the sides of your vehicle. But since most people haven't figured this out yet, they're still driving around with blind spots. And blind spots are deadly for motorcyclists. Never ride alongside the rear part of a car, because most likely the driver has no idea you are there. It's best not to ride beside any vehicle if you can help it, but if you have to ride beside one, at least make sure that you're riding in a spot where the other driver can see you if he or she bothers to look.

THE SOFT LANE CHANGE

SOMETIMES WE PRACTICE LIFESAVING techniques without even knowing we're doing them until someone explicitly points them out to us. This happened to me when I read about "the soft lane change" in a book called *Ride Hard, Ride Smart* (Motorbooks: 2004), written by a fellow named Pat Hahn who coordinates public information and education for the Minnesota Motorcycle Safety Center.

What Hahn means by "soft lane change" is easing into a lane when you're changing lanes rather than darting into the new lane. This will allow you and anyone else on the road time and space for mistakes. No matter how thoroughly you've checked the lane you plan to enter, there's always something you might have missed, like a car in the next lane over deciding to occupy that same lane, or some fool weaving through traffic at 100-plus miles per hour.

To perform a soft lane change, first check your mirrors and blind spot to make certain the lane you want to move into is clear (as you would anytime you change lanes). Next, signal your lane change (again, just as you would anytime you change lanes), but instead of moving from the center of the lane you're in to the center of the next lane, just move to the line that divides the two lanes and hold that position, leaving your turn signal on. Before you move all the way into the next lane, once again check your mirror and glance over at your blind spot to make certain you didn't miss something or that some kid with a fast car and a death wish isn't zigzagging through the lane.

Leave your turn signal on while you do this. If you've missed something and there's a car you didn't see, the driver should have realized your intentions by this point. The person will most likely either honk his or her horn at you or move over to let you in. Either option is better than getting hit by the other vehicle.

You'll complete the lane change only after you're absolutely certain that no other vehicle is vying for the same space. Don't turn off your turn signal until after you've safely completed the lane change. All of this should happen in a matter of seconds, which is a lot longer than you might think, but the extra time taken could mean the difference between you getting where you're going or you ending up in a hospital or a morgue.

You should practice soft lane changes not just every time you ride a motorcycle, but anytime you operate any vehicle on public roads. This is the surest way to avoid hitting hard-to-see vehicles while changing lanes, such as motorcycles, for example. If you always practice soft lane changes, the life you save may be my own.

PRESERVING SAFE SPACE

ON A BIKE YOU don't have fenders and bumpers and safety cages and crumple zones to protect you in case of an accident. Instead, you have flesh-and-blood legs and arms that are no match for three tons of sport utility vehicle. Because you are so vulnerable, you need to keep as much space as possible around you.

You do this by safely positioning your bike on the road. Always put your bike in the position that gives you the best view of the road ahead of you. Don't follow vehicles too closely, because in addition to blocking your view of the road ahead, tailgating takes away valuable time for you to react in an emergency. This is especially true when following a truck. If you find yourself following a truck, make sure to keep extra space between you and the truck. Better yet, make sure to choose a lane in which there are no vehicles in front of you, if that is at all possible.

If traffic is too heavy and there are no clear lanes available, stay to the right or the left of the lane so that you can see past the vehicles in front of you. Avoid riding in the center of the lane because in addition to affording the least visibility, that is the slipperiest part of the lane. Car engines, transmissions, and radiators are located between the car's wheels, and most of the slippery liquids that drip from a car on the highway build up in the center of the lane. The wheels that pass on the edges of the lane tend to keep the wheel tracks clean and free of slippery buildup, so you'll get your best traction there.

As you become more familiar with traffic patterns you'll learn to make traffic work for you instead of against you. On multilane roads you can position your bike in the right lane so that vehicles in the left lane will block oncoming drivers making left turns from hitting you. This is a skill that will require you to be able to read and assess a situation instantly, and you need to be confident of your riding skills and reaction times.

On occasion this will necessitate riding more aggressively than you might normally so you can keep up with fast-moving traffic, or even ride a little faster than the rest of traffic, but this isn't always a bad thing. Some studies have even shown that a motorcyclist riding just a bit faster than traffic is safer than a motorcyclist riding slower than traffic or even just the same speed as traffic. That seems to be the case in my experience.

This doesn't mean you'll have an excuse to ride as fast as you want. The key here is to ride *slightly* faster. As we mentioned earlier, deviating from traffic flow is a sure way to get into an accident. If you're riding slightly faster than traffic, you're doing so because you're trying to increase the safe space around your motorcycle. You're speeding up to move into a free space in traffic and avoid getting boxed in by other vehicles. Always try to find a spot in traffic that provides you with the most room possible. Sometimes this will mean you have to change lanes to find one with more safe space in which to ride, but that doesn't mean you'll be zipping in and out of traffic like a lunatic. You'll be changing lanes safely and sensibly, using the soft-lane-change method described in the last section.

Poor road conditions or poor weather conditions will require additional time to respond to unexpected events, so you'll need even more safe space in such conditions. You can get that safe space by slowing down, giving yourself more time to react. Debris on the road will also require you to slow down to give yourself more reaction time and thus more safe space.

You'll even need to be aware of the safe space around you when you park your motorcycle. Since motorcycles are so hard to see, someone might consider a parking space you're occupying empty and try to park in it. You may be standing there, putting on your helmet and gloves, and the next thing you know you're looking at the undercarriage of a Dodge Ram. When you pull into a parking space, position your motorcycle so that it is as visible to other drivers using the parking lot as possible.

BRAKING PRACTICE

ONE OF THE MOST dangerous situations in which you can find yourself is one in which you've locked up your brakes. At that point your tires have zero traction and the slightest twitch or sneeze or even blink on your part will put you down on the ground. The best you can hope for is a low-side, which is a crash where you just lay the bike down without flipping it over, but you're just as likely to go over the high side.

To avoid locking up your brakes, you need to know the traction limits of your bike, and the only way to really find out where those limits are is to test them. This practice itself is somewhat dangerous, but there are ways to do it that make it less dangerous. First off you'll need to find a safe place to practice, like a large, empty parking lot with clean, smooth pavement, somewhere where you can safely accelerate up to speeds of 20 to 30 miles per hour. Once you reach that speed, practice stopping as hard as you can. Remember that your front brake does most of the work.

Keep stopping harder and harder, and eventually you'll brake so hard that you lock up one of the tires. If your brakes are functioning properly, this will almost certainly be the rear tire. Immediately ease pressure on the brake pedal until the tire is once again turning freely. If you were only going 20 to 30 miles an hour when you started, you should have slowed down enough by the time the rear wheel locks to avoid crashing.

Once you're accustomed to using both brakes hard, practice the same drill using just the front brake. At the slightest hint of the front tire locking up, release the front brake. If you lock up your front brake, you will most likely fall down, even at low speeds. Once you've got a feel for this, go back to practicing with both brakes. You'll notice that your stops are both shorter and more controlled, even after just a few practice stops.

Do this several times, and by the time you're finished, you'll be able to feel what your motorcycle is doing just before you lock up your brakes. Your hands and feet will tell you when a tire is about to lock up. This will help give you an instinctive sense for just how much braking force you can apply in a real emergency situation.

Braking is such an important skill that you need to keep practicing it, even after you've mastered the basics. When you're out on the open road approaching stop signs, first make certain that no one is behind you. Once you've determined the road behind you is clear, practice stopping hard on different types of roads and road surfaces. Don't brake to the point of locking up your tires, but do try to stop in as little distance as possible. That way when a deer jumps out in front of you or some fool doesn't see you and pulls out on the highway just as you're approaching an intersection, hard stops will be second nature for you. Instead of panicking and having a life-threatening crash, your instincts will take over and you'll be much more likely to come to a safe stop.

RIDING IN THE RAIN

IF YOU RIDE A motorcycle, you will get caught in bad weather, even if you live in the desert. It's part of the deal you make with the world when you decide to become a motorcyclist. If you prepare properly and know what you're doing, it's not as terrible as you might think. But riding in the rain does increase your danger level.

Having a good rain suit helps to reduce some of the danger. If you're warm and dry rather than wet, cold, and miserable, you'll be much more focused on the matter at hand, which is, of course, safely riding your motorcycle. Rain suits are either one- or two-piece suits made of polyvinyl chloride (PVC) or nylon. The one-piece suits do a better job of keeping a rider dry because they don't allow rain to seep in at a rider's waist, the way a two-piece suit can. On the other hand, the two-piece suits are easier to put on quickly at the side of the road.

Polyvinyl chloride provides better protection from the rain than does nylon, but it's sticky to the touch, especially when wet, making it hard to put on over leather. Because of this a good PVC suit will have a cotton mesh lining that slides against leather riding gear. Ideally both the top and bottom of the suit should be mesh-lined. The better the rain gear, the more it will cost, but in this case you really do get what you pay for.

Staying dry in the rain is just part of the battle. You also have to stay up on two wheels. You have a lot less traction available on wet roads than on dry roads, which equates to much less traction available for turning and stopping. That means you have to slow down when you're riding in the rain, and you have to be even smoother when using the throttle and brakes than when you are on dry pavement. Jerky steering or throttle inputs that you wouldn't even notice on dry pavement can put you down on the ground when the road is wet.

Earlier I mentioned that you should avoid riding in the center of the lane because that's where all the slippery fluids build up. When it rains, the water lifts these fluids up off the pavement and makes them even slipperier, so it's especially important to avoid the center of the lane when it's raining. What's problematic about this is that pavement often sinks down in the wheel tracks where you ride, allowing water to build up in them. This can lead to hydroplaning, which is an extremely low-traction situation.

This is the main reason you want to make sure that you have a lot of tread on your tires; the more your tires wear down, the shallower the rain grooves cut into their surface become. These grooves allow water to squeeze out from under your tires as you ride, keeping the tire rubber in contact with the pavement. As your tires start to become bald, the water begins to build up under them when you ride in the rain. This is what causes hydroplaning.

The trend toward fatter tires seems to have made motorcycles more susceptible to hydroplaning. While riding across Texas on my way to Minnesota for a club rally in the summer of 2009 my bike hydroplaned in a rainstorm. Since the tires had good tread on them, I think the culprit might have been the size of the tires, which are exceptionally fat.

What You Should Know

- After receiving initial rider training, the best thing you can do to ensure your survival as a motorcyclist is to get advanced training.
- Everyone else on the road has the potential to kill you at any time.
- Situational awareness at all times is the key to staying alive on a motorcycle.

CHAPTER SEVEN

LIVING WITH A MOTORCYCLE

Now that you've learned enough about motorcycles to decide what type you want, you've learned how to ride, and you've bought a motorcycle, I'm going to give you some advice on what to do with it. This is the fun stuff. I'm going to talk a bit about traveling and about joining clubs. But first I'm going to discuss some basic motorcycle maintenance, which might not sound like much fun, but when you develop a bond with your motorcycle, you'll learn to enjoy it (or at least not hate it).

Figuring out what to do with your motorcycle isn't that complicated. First and foremost, you'll just want to get out there and ride the wheels off your new bike. After you first start to ride, your motorcycle will become your obsession. When you're not riding it, you're sneaking out to the garage to polish and maintain it. If you're anything like me, you'll continue to feel this way long after the new wears off your motorcycle. I've been riding for nearly sixty years, and I still can't wait to get out on my bike. As soon as I finish writing this chapter, I plan to head straight for my garage to take my bike out for a ride.

Before you ever hit the road on your motorcycle, you'll want to make sure that it's in top working order. I apologize for going back to the dark side of motorcycling for a moment here, but the consequences of just one bolt coming loose while you're riding are so horrible that you don't want to leave anything to chance.

When I started riding, it seemed like we practically had to rebuild our motorcycles every time we took them out on the road. In fact, it was like this until not all that long ago. Motorcycle technology has come a long way in the past thirty years and today's motorcycles are more like modern cars when it comes to maintenance requirements, but they still need more maintenance than any car. You'll still need to perform routine procedures to keep your bike in safe condition.

BASIC MAINTENANCE

PEOPLE HAVE STRONG FEELINGS about motorcycle maintenance—it seems like they either love it or hate it. I have to admit that I'm not particularly fond of it, but like it or not, I've spent a good chunk of my life wrenching on motorcycles. Today I can afford to have a good mechanic maintain my bike and I don't miss doing it myself. Still, I'm glad I learned how to work on a motorcycle because even today's reliable motorcycles break down now and then.

Because of that, I recommend that you learn how to do basic maintenance and repair on your motorcycle. I'm not saying you need to go to some motorcycle mechanics program to learn how to overhaul your own machine; I'm talking about basic routine maintenance that anyone can do.

Before you start working on your bike you should get a repair manual of some sort. Most new bikes will have instructions for basic maintenance in their owner's manual, though sometimes they'll say that the job should only be performed by technicians trained for that brand of bike. I think that's chickenshit, but I guess manufacturers don't much care what I think. They probably give more weight to what their lawyers think because they're afraid of being held liable if some fool does something stupid. Protecting fools from themselves seems a futile activity to me, but I digress.

Your owner's manual will most likely be insufficient if you want to work on your own motorcycle. If you bought your bike used, you may not even have an owner's manual. You'll have to supplement your owner's manual with some sort of repair manual. Clymer, Haynes, and Chilton all publish generic repair manuals for most motorcycles. These are usually adequate, though they're not ideal because they tend to cover families of bikes rather than specific models, and they don't always do a good job addressing small differences between different models.

Your best option would be to buy an actual shop repair manual for your bike. These are the manuals that the manufacturers publish for their own mechanics to use. They cover every detail of your bike, from removing bodywork to tearing down an engine. These will give you all the tricks you need to know to work on your particular machine. Sometimes something that seems as simple as removing a series of bolts can go from an uncomplicated job to a complete nightmare if you remove the bolts in the wrong order. The repair manual will provide you with that sort of inside information. Repair manuals are expensive and can run up to $100 apiece, or even more, but if you plan to do any complicated work on your own bike, that is money well spent.

The first things you'll need to work on your bike are some basic tools. Most Japanese and European bikes come with tool kits. The Japanese tool kits generally aren't very good and won't be sufficient for even routine maintenance. BMWs come with high-quality tool kits. Triumph tool kits aren't quite as good as BMW kits, but they're much better than the ones that come with Japanese bikes. Harleys don't come with tool kits at all.

I suggest putting together your own small tool kit that fits in the saddlebags. At the very least you'll need the following items in your tool kit:

- **Wrench set.** This will be your most important tool, so get the highest-quality wrenches you can. If you're trying to save space, you can get open-ended wrenches that have different-sized wrenches on each end. If you have bigger saddlebags, you can get wrenches that have open ends on one side and boxed ends on the other. If your bike uses metric-sized bolts and nuts, get a metric set. If it uses SAE standard-sized nuts and bolts, get an SAE standard wrench set.

- **Ratchet and socket set.** As with your wrenches, make sure you get the correct type, either metric or SAE standard. I have a compact ratchet with a three-quarter-inch drive and an articulating elbow in my tool kit. This is handy for getting at bolts and nuts in hard-to-reach places. And it is sufficient for minor maintenance and repair, but the articulating joint would make it unsuitable for major repair jobs.

  In addition to the ratchet, I keep sockets in all the most common sizes. I also recommend getting at least one extension for the sockets. If you only get one, it's better to get a longer one than a short one, but ideally you should have two or three extensions of different lengths. You might only keep the medium one in your on-bike tool kit and keep the others in your garage tool kit.

- **Screwdrivers.** To save space, I have a screwdriver with replaceable tips and keep a variety of tips in both Phillips and flat-blade sizes. If you have a Harley, you'll also want to get a Torx screwdriver. This has a star-shaped tip and is the only way to remove some screws on Harleys. You can also get these with multiple tips.

  Don't skimp and try to get by with cheap screwdrivers. And throw out screwdrivers as soon as they start to wear out. If you have rounded tips on your screwdrivers, you'll strip screw heads, turning a simple job into an expensive trip to a machine shop to have a stripped screw drilled out. If it's an important screw, it may even require you to tow your bike to the shop. One tow trip to the shop would pay for a lifetime of screwdrivers.

- **Allen wrench set.** You can usually get one Allen wrench that contains all the different sizes you need folded up like a pocketknife. Remember to get the right type for your bike: metric or SAE standard.

- **Pliers.** Ideally you'll want both regular and needle-nose pliers, but if you only have room for one, I'd go with the needle-nose pliers. I used to recommend regular pliers but have changed my mind because needle-nose pliers are more versatile. Needle-nose pliers can do pretty much anything regular pliers can do, although they aren't very good at things like removing bolts. But needle-nose pliers can do many things that regular pliers can't. Besides, if you have your wrenches and sockets, you should use those for removing bolts and nuts instead of pliers.

- **Spark-plug wrench.** The best spark-plug wrench is a deep-well socket that you can use on your ratchet, but make sure your socket is deep enough to get down to the bolt lugs on your spark plug.

- **Air pressure gauge.** Get a good-quality gauge that provides an accurate reading. I prefer a dial gauge because it's more accurate, it's easier to use in tight spaces, and also because it takes up less space in my tool kit than a traditional pencil-type gauge.

In addition to your portable tool kit, you should have a few basic tools at home in your garage:

- **A stool.** It doesn't hurt to squat beside your bike for a moment or two, but most jobs take longer than you expect. Your legs will get sore in a hurry if you squat beside your motorcycle for any length of time. You might even do permanent nerve damage. It's much more comfortable to sit on a stool while you're working.

- **A torque wrench.** This is a wrench that measures how tightly a nut has been twisted onto a bolt. It does this by either having a needle that points to the torque value, or a ratchet-type device that freewheels when a nut has been torqued to the proper specification. Your repair manual will have a proper torque value for just about every fastener on your bike. It's especially important to get the proper torque on things like axle bolts and triple-clamp bolts. If they are too loose, your wheels or fork could fall off; if they are too tight, your bearings will wear prematurely.

- **An oil filter wrench.** This will be a wrench that either wraps around the body of your oil filter with bands that tighten as you turn the wrench or else a cap that you place on the bottom of the filter itself and turn with a ratchet (and usually a long extension).

- **A soft-faced mallet.** You'll often run into a situation where some stubborn part needs a little persuasion. The trouble is you can't bang on these parts with just any tool or you'll damage them. A soft-faced mallet will allow you to use the required amount of force without damaging the part in question.

- **Lubricants.** At the very least you'll need engine oil and some WD-40. If you have a bike with a chain final drive, you'll also need some chain lube (don't use WD-40 on your chain—see the upcoming "Maintaining Your Chain" section for details).

- **Funnels.** You'll need a variety of funnels of different sizes and different-length spouts to reach all the places in which you'll need to get fluid into a motorcycle. You can also use them to catch the fluids you're removing from a motorcycle, especially motorcycles with dry-sump engines and remote oil tanks, like older Harleys (and current-model Sportsters). You'll want funnels made of different types of material, as some applications will call for a stiff funnel made of aluminum, whereas others will require a pliable plastic funnel.

- **Containers.** You'll want a red plastic can to hold fresh gas, and you'll want a small spray can to spray oil or small amounts of gas. You'll also want a fairly large catch pan to catch the oil you drain from your engine when you're performing an oil change, and larger covered containers in which to store the oil until you can get it to a recycling center.

CHANGING OIL

ENGINE OIL TECHNOLOGY HAS developed at almost the same breakneck pace as motorcycle technology, and the oils we have today are much better than the oils we had available even thirty years ago. All the major brands are very good, though you need to make sure that you use the oil weight specified by your bike's manufacturer. But as good as modern oil has become, you'll still need to change it on a regular basis. I prefer to err on the side of caution and change oil every twenty-five hundred miles, even though I use high-quality oil.

The following is a general outline of what's involved in changing engine oil. I'm not going to go into the preparation needed to ready your bike for an oil change, like removing bodywork, because the process will vary from bike to bike so there's no way to cover it here. On some bikes you might not even have to remove bodywork. I know a guy with a sport bike who removes just one bolt from his inner fairing and that lets him pull the fairing out far enough so that he can get the oil to drain straight down into his oil pan. You'll have to figure out how to get access to your own drain plug and oil filter. After that, you'll use the following procedure:

1. **Wear good latex gloves.** This isn't just to keep your hands pretty. We know for a fact that oil is a carcinogen, and you don't want it to touch your skin.
2. **Run the engine for a short time to warm up the oil.** This makes changing oil a potentially

painful experience, but you'll need the oil to be warm to flow freely out of the engine. Note that this will make your exhaust pipes extremely hot, so be careful not to touch them when you're working on your bike.

3. **Locate the drain plug.** The drain plug will be somewhere on the sump at the bottom of your motorcycle engine, or else on the bottom edge of one side. Once you've located it, place your catch pan under the plug. (If you have a dry sump with an external oil tank, like the one on a Harley Sportster, you'll have to drain the oil tank instead of the sump.)

4. **Remove the plug.** This is usually a large, hex-head bolt. Let the oil drain completely into the catch pan. Be careful when you remove the plug because the hot oil will pour out over your fingers. You'll need to pull the plug away from the hole quickly once you've unscrewed it or you could burn your fingers. Be especially careful not to drop the plug into the catch pan or you'll have to fish it out of a pan of hot, dirty oil.

5. **Clean and replace the drain plug once the oil has finished draining from the engine.** Most drain plugs have magnetic tips that collect metal shavings from inside the engine. Clean all of this material off before replacing the plug. Some drain plugs have metal washers to enhance the plug's seal. If your bike is so equipped, make certain you don't lose this washer when removing the plug. Also make certain the area around the hole is clean and doesn't have any dirt or debris that could get inside your engine or pre-

vent the drain plug from forming a seal against the oil pan.

6. **Place the catch pan under the oil filter and remove it.** You'll want to change the filter every time you change oil, so consider that a normal part of changing oil. Older bikes use canister-type filters, which are elements that go inside a canister that's permanently attached to the engine, but most modern motorcycles use automotive-type spin-on filters.

   Again, watch out for hot oil spraying down on your hand. The old filter will be filled with engine oil—dump this in the catch pan and properly dispose of the filter.

7. **Attach the new filter.** Smear clean engine oil from the bottles you're using to refill the engine sump onto the rubber seal attached to the top of the new filter, then screw it back on the engine. Only use your hands to tighten the filter—don't use the filter wrench or you'll get the filter so tight you may never be able to remove it again.

8. **Refill the oil.** As mentioned earlier, different bikes use different methods for measuring the oil level. Make sure that you fill the oil tank to the top of the level using the measuring method specified for your bike. Once you've got it to the full mark, restart the engine to pump oil into the filter.

   Be careful when you are doing this. When you first start the engine, your oil system won't be pressurized for the first couple seconds, so if you rev the engine, you could do permanent damage. Let the engine idle for a minute or two, then shut it down and recheck the oil. The oil level will have gone down by the amount that has been pumped into the filter. Refill the oil to the full mark.

After you've changed your oil, keep an eye on the oil level and check for leaks around the drain plug and the filter the next few times you ride the bike, just in case something has gone wrong.

MAINTAINING YOUR CHAIN

I THINK I'VE MADE my feelings about chain drives clear throughout the book, but if your budget only allows you to buy a midpriced motorcycle, most likely you'll have to settle for a chain-driven bike. That means you'll have to deal with the hassle of maintaining a chain. And you'll have to do this yourself because if you take it in to a shop to have the chain tightened, well, your bike will be in the shop all the time.

Replacing chains and sprockets, on the other hand, is a huge job, one that you probably will want to leave to a trained mechanic unless you're fairly skilled. The chores you'll handle yourself will be cleaning, lubricating, and tightening the tension of your chain.

Chains are expensive so you'll want to make them last as long as possible. This means you'll want to keep them clean and well lubricated. Most modern chains have internal lubrication permanently sealed in place with rubber O-rings. This makes the chains last longer, but it also means that you have to be careful what kind of products you use on them, since some chemicals will degrade the O-rings. This means you should not use WD-40. WD-40 is an excellent product for its intended use, but it is a penetrating lubricant used to loosen up things like tight bolts. WD-40 will penetrate the O-rings, destroying their seals. To clean the grime off your chain, only use an O-ring compatible cleaner and a soft brush.

Lubricate the chain with one of the many excellent chain lubricants on the market. I've heard good things about both Bel-Ray and PJ1 brands. Lubricating the chain is best done while the motorcycle is up on the center stand or up on a good support stand like a Pit Bull. When you apply the lubricant, aim the spray from the can at the inside of the chain, just ahead of the rear sprocket, while rotating the wheel forward to evenly coat the chain. This will not only lubricate the chain but also the rear sprocket, which is exposed and needs better lubricant coverage than does the front sprocket, which is covered and somewhat protected from dirt and debris. When you've lubricated the entire chain, clean the excess lubricant off the wheel and tire.

Ideally you'll want to check your chain's tension while someone is sitting aboard your bike, holding it up but putting his or her weight on the suspension so that the springs are compressed. It would be best if the person weighed as close as possible to your weight. This will put your suspension at the angle at which it will be when you're riding and will give you the most accurate reading of your chain's tension. I say this because the distance between the front and rear sprockets changes as the angle between the swingarm and the engine changes. This change in distance is extremely slight, but it can be enough to affect the tension of the chain. Checking the tension with the swingarm at the proper angle can help prevent you from overtightening your chain; overtightening is the main killer of chains.

To check the tension, grasp the chain on the underside of the swingarm about halfway between the front and rear sprockets and move the chain up and down. If the chain moves up and down more than about an inch and a half or two inches, it needs to be tightened. Check in several different spots on the chain by rolling the bike ahead and rechecking the tension. If the amount of chain movement varies from place to place, the chain may have a tight spot. If the tight spot is bad enough, you'll have to replace the chain. A tight spot is simply a spot where the chain is stiff and doesn't bend on its roller pins. Note that a "tight spot" is different than having a chain that is too tight.

The chain-tightening procedure varies from bike to bike, but most chain-driven motorcycles will use some form of the following method to adjust chain tension. Place the bike on its center stand or on the portable stand you've purchased and recheck the chain's tension. It will have changed from when you checked it while the suspension was weighted because the distance between the front and rear sprocket will have changed. It will feel looser than it did while the other person was sitting on the bike. If it moved an inch and a half while the suspension was weighted, it might move three inches when the suspension is unweighted.

Take this into account when adjusting the chain so you don't overtighten it. If you gained an inch and a half of chain travel by putting the bike on the stand and then tighten the chain down to an appropriate three-quarters of an inch of travel, your chain will be stretched as tight as a funeral drum when you get back on your bike. This will stretch your chain and drastically decrease its life span. Overtightening to this degree may even cause your chain to break and shoot off the back of your sprocket like a missile.

To prevent this catastrophe, add the amount of chain travel you gained when you put the bike up on the stand to the three-quarters of an inch you need for proper operation. If you gained an inch and a half of travel when you put the bike up on the stand, don't tighten your chain beyond two to two and a quarter inches of travel. This should put you right in the half inch to three-quarters of an inch of travel that you need when you get back on the bike.

Next, loosen the axle nuts. You will have to remove a security pin on most bikes when loosening the axle nuts. Once the axle nuts are removed, you can adjust the chain. You do this by adjusting bolts on the end of the swingarm on either side of the wheel. Usually there will be two hex-head nuts on each bolt—an inner nut to move the axle and an outer nut to lock the inner nut in place when the job is done. Loosen up the outer nut and then carefully adjust the inner nut, moving the nut on one side of the wheel a small amount, then moving the other nut an equal amount. If you don't move the bolts on each side the exact same amount, your back tire will get out of alignment with your front tire. When you've got the tension set to the proper amount, tighten down the outside nuts to lock the inner nuts in place. Retighten the axle bolts and insert a new security pin.

TOURING

FROM THE FIRST TIME I got on a motorcycle, I had the urge to take off and keep on riding. I still do. I like riding everywhere—to the store, to the gym, wherever—but there's nothing I enjoy as much as hitting the open road for a long trip. I hope you'll share my enthusiasm for long-distance riding.

You can travel on any bike you own, if it is reliable. Some bikes make better touring rides than others, but ultimately the best bike for a tour is the one sitting in your garage, because that's what you've got available. You might as well make the most of it. If you've followed my advice, you've bought a bike that is comfortable. If that's the case, the only real functional issues you'll have to deal with are luggage capacity and fuel range.

Having a bike with too small a gas tank can be a real hindrance to successful touring. Most bikes available today have at least sufficient fuel capacity to prevent you from being stranded between gas stops, but that wasn't always the case. For many years Harley-Davidson Sportsters had notoriously small gas tanks. This was such a serious problem that you didn't want to head out of town by yourself on a Sportster for fear of running out of gas and being stranded. Today's Sportsters still have small tanks that make them poorly suited for long-distance travel, but at least they're large enough for you to make it to the next gas station without running out of fuel most of the time. (There have been other bikes with such small fuel tanks that they have been all but impossible to use for touring, including Kawasaki's Eliminator of the mid-1980s and Honda's Superhawk of the late 1990s, but most of the bikes on the market today have fuel capacity that is at least adequate.)

You can't do much about your bike's fuel capacity without radical modification, but you can alter your bike's luggage capacity without too much trouble. Lots of luggage options are available that will work on almost any motorcycle. The trick is to equip your bike with luggage that stays securely fastened and doesn't rub against your tires or belt or chain.

If you've bought a bike equipped with saddlebags, you're already three-quarters of the way to having all the luggage capacity you'll need. If you have a touring bike, you might even have a top box or trunk on the back. If you like the hard luggage found on a touring bike, you may be able to buy optional hard luggage specifically for your bike, either from the manufacturer or from an aftermarket company like Givi or Corbin. This is the best way to go, but it's also an expensive route and will probably require you to put your motorcycle in a shop for a day or two while the luggage is installed.

If you don't have the money, time, or patience to go this route, you can mount soft luggage. There are three basic pieces of soft luggage:

- **Saddlebags.** These are bags that you put over the rear portion of your seat and ride outboard of the rear wheel, one on each side of the bike. These are usually your primary piece of luggage.

- **Tankbags.** These are bags that mount on top of your tank. They can hold a lot of items and provide the easiest access for a rider in the saddle. They make great places to store items you frequently need while riding, like cameras, sunscreen, bottled water, and fluid and soft rags for cleaning your face shield. Plus they're handy for storing articles of clothing you might remove as the temperature warms up during the day, like sweatshirts and heavy gloves.

- **Tailpacks.** These mount on the passenger portion of your seat and can greatly increase your luggage capacity, making them invaluable for long trips. The best of these will have built-in bungee cords so you can securely attach them to your bike.

Soft removable saddlebags can be made of leather, vinyl, or heavy nylon. Tankbags and tailpacks are almost always made of heavy nylon, though some have hard plastic shells. Soft luggage has its drawbacks. It's not lockable, like hard luggage, and you have to be careful to mount the pieces securely so they don't move around and rub your tires or fall off. Removable soft luggage also isn't rainproof, meaning that you'll have to pack your stuff in heavy garbage bags before you put it in the luggage, but it has the advantages of being inexpensive and easily removed when you are done traveling.

PACKING FOR A TRIP

ALMOST EVERY PERSON WHO takes his or her first motorcycle trip makes the same mistake: packing too
much gear. You'll overload your luggage with stuff
that you won't even unpack until you get back home.
Everyone with any touring experience will warn you
not to do this, but you'll do it anyway because you'll
be worried that you'll need this or that item but won't
have it.

Really, you only need a few items for a safe, comfortable trip. Bring the small tool kit I told you about
earlier in this chapter, of course. Bring a first-aid kit,
too. It doesn't have to be elaborate, but should include the following basic items:

- A selection of bandages, including gauze bandages
- Adhesive tape
- Some sort of antibiotic

If you have room to add a few more items, you
should try to fit them in. Your first-aid kit isn't the
place to save weight.

Apply the less-is-more philosophy in spades when
it comes to your clothes. Bring a couple of pairs of
jeans, a few T-shirts, a couple of turtleneck sweaters
(turtleneck sweaters are great in cold weather because
they make a nice seal between your jacket and your
helmet). Bring enough underwear and socks to last
you the duration of your trip (underwear and socks
don't take up much space). That about covers it. As
long as you have clean underwear and socks, you can
get by in most situations.

Traveling on a motorcycle is one of the most rewarding activities in which you can ever engage. It is also one of the most grueling. Spending a long day in the saddle takes the piss right out of you. You're going to have to prepare your body as much as you prepare your gear and your bike.

I recommend starting an exercise regime before going on a motorcycle trip. This will help build up your stamina and endurance. And get in the habit of eating a healthy diet. This will be hard to keep up when you're out on the road, eating in restaurants every day, but if you make smart choices, you can keep your energy level high. The most important thing is to drink enough water. If you just drink soda or coffee, the caffeine in those drinks depletes your body's water supply. Get in the habit of drinking a bottle of water each time you stop for gas.

PLANNING A TRIP

WHEN YOU PLAN YOUR first trip, you'll probably spend weeks, or even months poring over maps, plotting your route. Chances are that you will have fun, but the odds are just as good that you'll bite off more than you can chew. Most people underestimate how much time their trips will take, which leads them to rush to make up time. If you fall into this trap, you'll miss seeing a lot of the things you wanted to see in the first place. Plus you'll be anxious and won't be able to relax and enjoy the trip itself.

The trick for avoiding this pitfall is to be realistic when planning your trip in the first place. If your route will take you across South Dakota or some other state where the interstate speed limit is 75 miles per hour, don't expect to cover seventy-five miles for every hour you're out on your bike, even if you're riding at 80 miles per hour or faster. You need to factor in things like gas stops, rest stops, and getting stuck behind the occasional semi. At best, you'll probably average 60 miles per hour.

As you become more experienced, your average speed will increase, but not by much. If you're riding two-up or riding with a group of bikes, you'll probably average even slower. When you're with a group of bikers, rest stops take longer because more people are using the available bathrooms, gas stops take longer because more tanks need to be filled, and riding itself takes longer because not everyone travels at the same speed. Ultimately you'll only travel as fast as the slowest rider in the group.

Thus if you plan to spend eight hours traveling by yourself on a freeway (which is a long time to be droning down a long, straight interstate highway), don't expect to cover more than four hundred miles that day. And you won't be able to make up time by speeding because those few minutes you might gain by riding faster will be more than lost by the half hour or more that you'll sit alongside the road while the state trooper calls in your license information and writes your expensive speeding ticket.

If you're riding on two-lane highways, you can knock your average speed down to 50 miles per hour because the speed limits will be lower and you'll spend more time being cock blocked by traffic. If you get into the mountains where the roads turn twisty and the scenic beauty beckons you to stop and take photos, figure that at best you'll cover thirty to forty miles every hour, and less if you're with a group of other bikers. You could push yourself and not stop to enjoy the scenery, but that defeats the purpose of being there on a motorcycle in the first place. It's better to take your time and enjoy your trip than to turn it into the Bataan Death March.

If you are worried about not covering enough ground, it's better to plan a shorter trip. If you are going to some destination, like to visit a relative in a far-off state, don't try to cram in a lot of sightseeing and side trips. If you have to be somewhere quickly, you won't be able to stop and enjoy the extra places you're visiting anyway. If you don't have to be anywhere at any specific time, plan shorter routes that allow you plenty of time to absorb the places you visit. If you are going to spend five days riding through Colorado and Wyoming, don't plan a trip that will cover more than fifteen hundred miles.

Whatever you do, don't run yourself ragged while you're traveling on a bike. Relax, get plenty of sleep, and eat a healthy diet. Make sure you take time to stop and stretch your legs when you visit someplace or stop to take some photos. You might not think it's possible to fall asleep while riding a bike, but it is, and the potential consequences range from horrible to even worse. Even if you don't fall asleep, the more tired you are, the less alert you are. The less alert you are, the slower your reaction times. The slower your reaction times, the more likely you are to get killed. If you compare the potential costs of pushing yourself while on a trip with any potential benefits, you'll see that there's nothing to be gained by rushing your trip and everything to lose.

CLUBS

As MOST OF YOU probably knew before you picked up this book, I'm a member of a motorcycle club. It's the type of club that's often called a "one-percenter" club. As the legend goes, an AMA spokesperson once said that 99 percent of all motorcyclists were good, responsible citizens, and all the trouble was being caused by the 1 percent of outlaws. I have my own ideas about this. I was there for a lot of the so-called trouble, and to me it seemed like there was a disconnection between what was really happening and what the press was reporting. I'd attend an event in which nothing out of the ordinary appeared to happen, and then I'd read a sensationalized account of that same event in the press in which it seemed that all the barbaric tribes of Europe had descended. My take is that most of the trouble referred to by this AMA official, if he even existed, took place in the pages of newspapers and magazines, and not in the flesh-and-blood world.

Regardless, the one-percent title stuck and actually became a badge of honor for club members. We consider one-percenter clubs elite organizations, where membership isn't open to just anyone. Membership requires extreme dedication. When you become a member of a one-percenter club, the club becomes your life. It becomes your family—your parents, your brothers and sisters, your wife, and your children.

When you become a member of a one-percenter club, you have dedicated your life to that club.

As far as I'm concerned, extreme dedication is what separates one-percenter clubs from other types of clubs, but there are certain characteristics that are shared by many (but not all) one-percenter clubs. Most one-percenter club members wear some sort of garment that features the club patch (often called "colors") centered on the back of the garment, where it can be seen while the man (as politically incorrect as this may be, there are no one-percenter clubs that allow women to be members—clubs that allow women are by nature not one-percenter clubs) is riding his motorcycle. That garment is usually a denim vest, or more accurately, a denim jacket with the sleeves cut off, which is why it's often called a "cut," but sometimes the patch is sewn on a leather vest or jacket.

Typically a one-percenter patch consists of three parts: a central image depicting the club's insignia, a rocker patch (a curved bar) on top with the club's name, and another rocker patch below indicating the particular chapter of a club. This type of three-piece patch usually signifies that a club is a one-percenter club, but not always. I'll soon explain that in more detail. Likewise if a patch is a two-piece or one-piece patch, that usually means that the club is not a one-percenter club.

One-percenter clubs are as varied as the individuals who make up their memberships. Some clubs consist of single groups located in a specific geographic area whereas others are composed of chapters spread around the country, or even the globe. Few one-percenter clubs recruit their members. Instead, the clubs attract prospective members by their public behavior and reputation. We don't recruit; we recognize. Riders who aspire to be members approach the club, show their interest, and work to prove they are worthy.

The process a prospect follows usually goes as follows: introduction, hang-around status, sponsorship, prospect phase, and finally either membership or failure. The would-be prospect first reaches the provisional status of a "hang-around." This is when club members have privately voted to make official the hang-around's status of club associate.

If and when a club member deems the hang-around worthy of sponsorship as a prospect and is willing to act as the person's mentor, that member meets with the individual and offers to sponsor him. At a club meeting, the member stands up for the potential prospect and asks for a vote authorizing "prospect" status. By doing this the member becomes responsible for the prospect. If a majority of members agree, the prospect is brought into the meeting, told of his new status, and given the bottom rocker "prospect" patch.

The official recognition as "prospect" marks the beginning of the prospect's hard-core testing phase, which may take many months. The prospect is given menial tasks, such as cleaning the clubhouse, helping set up for meetings and events, running errands, and maintaining members' bikes. Occasionally he is also trusted with more significant jobs that require greater skill, creativity, or finesse; these assignments will come directly from the prospect's sponsor, upon whom the quality of the prospect's performance will reflect.

When the sponsoring member deems the time appropriate, he brings the prospect's membership to a vote before the whole club. This milestone event will include an open discussion among the members regarding the prospect's qualities (pro and con). In most clubs, a unanimous vote is required to grant membership. When the vote is taken, if only one member votes against granting membership, that member must explain his reasons in case he knows something the others do not.

If the members do not grant membership at this time, they decide whether to continue the prospect phase or dismiss the prospect entirely. If they do agree to make the prospect a member, they may invite the person into the meeting to congratulate him, or they may keep it a secret so they can surprise the prospect with his full patch at another time.

MOM-AND-POP CLUBS

DON'T FEEL BAD IF the life of a one-percenter isn't right for you. I have my priorities, and my club is at the top of that list, but because of that I've had to make a lot of sacrifices. I've never been able to have children because my club responsibilities are so demanding that I wouldn't have time to properly raise them. I've even gone to prison.

Like I said, one-percenter clubs are as varied as the individuals who compose them. The clubs are not criminal syndicates. Anytime you have a group of people collected together, the group will include some people who don't always abide by the letter of the law. You'd think that law-enforcement agencies would deal with individual club members on an individual basis, but you'd be wrong. All members of one-percenter clubs are painted with the same brush by law-enforcement agencies.

If you do join a one-percenter club, you'd better be prepared to live your life under a microscope. When you do any business transaction whatsoever, you'll need to make sure you have all your legal bases covered. This is part of the dedication required to be a member, and it's no easy thing.

But if you're interested in this type of club, only at a less-intense level, there are organizations that offer much of the brotherhood and camaraderie of a one-percenter club, and even elements of the one-percenter lifestyle, but that aren't actual one-percenter clubs. I guess you could call them "two-percenter" clubs. We call them "mom-and-pop" clubs. These clubs can be organized around riding motorcycles, like the one-percenter clubs, or they can be organized around something else. For example, there are two-percenter clubs that combine sobriety with motorcycling, clubs that combine religion with motorcycling, and even clubs composed of war veterans and police officers.

These clubs vary in the degree of dedication they require of their members. In general, if clubs use a three-piece patch, they'll require more dedication because usually they'll need to have an understanding with and abide by the rules set by the local one-percenter clubs in order to fly three-piece colors. Be warned: membership in one of the more dedicated mom-and-pop clubs may mean you'll suffer the same prejudice from the law-enforcement community as membership in a one-percenter club, especially at the local level. The FBI might know the difference between a church-based club or a group of Alcoholics Anonymous members and a real one-percenter club, but your local cop probably won't.

CLUBS FOR THE OTHER NINETY-EIGHT PERCENT

AGAIN, DON'T WORRY IF even these two-percenter clubs don't sound right for you. There are almost as many different types of motorcycle clubs as there are different types of motorcyclists. I highly recommend that you find one that suits your lifestyle and personality.

As a motorcyclist, you may often find yourself the odd man (or woman) out as you ride through the world. Although more and more of us are riding every year, we're still a very small minority of motorists. Clubs offer camaraderie and brotherhood. They provide social outlets, places where we can gather with our own kind and talk about our passion—motorcycles and riding—without boring nonmotorcyclists. A motorcycle club is a nexus where the motorcycling community can come together.

You can find a club devoted to every different type of riding. There are off-road and trail-riding clubs, there are road-racing and sport-bike clubs, and there are clubs devoted to long-distance touring riders. There are general clubs devoted to all motorcycles and clubs devoted to specific types of motorcycles, like turbocharged bikes. There are clubs devoted to antique motorcycles, and clubs devoted to every brand of motorcycle ever built, from ATK to Zundapp. In addition to clubs devoted to certain makes, there are clubs devoted to just specific models of those brands. Take BMW motorcycles, for example. There are clubs devoted to all BMW motorcycles, clubs devoted to just antique BMWs, clubs devoted to air-cooled BMWs, and clubs devoted to specific BMW models, like the GS series.

There are clubs devoted to riders from a particular area, clubs devoted to riders based on their sexual orientation, and clubs devoted to just one sex. For example, the Dykes on Bikes club is based on both sex and sexual orientation. There are clubs just for riders over a certain age, and there are clubs that no rider of a certain age would join if he or she was in his or her right mind. There are clubs based on every spiritual system known to man, from the Anglican Church to Zoroastrianism. There are clubs for everyone from Baptists to Buddhists. There are professionally oriented motorcycle clubs, such as clubs for cops and for firefighters, and I'm sure there are clubs just for slackers and bums.

Find out where motorcyclists gather, and ride there to check out the local scene. At the very least you'll meet people who share a powerful common interest with you: motorcycling. To find a club, or at least a loosely organized motorcycling community, all you really have to do is pursue the activity you most enjoy: riding a motorcycle.

What You Need to Know

- You need to learn to perform basic maintenance on your own bike, especially if it's chain-driven.
- You need to prepare your body and your bike for the rigors of a long trip.
- Joining a club is a great way to connect with the motorcycle community.

APPENDIX

Motorcycle Resources

MOTORCYCLE SAFETY FOUNDATION

THROUGHOUT THE BOOK I'VE referred to a variety of organizations, businesses, and other resources that I use and recommend. I'm presenting them here in alphabetical order because they are all more or less equally important, with one exception: the Motorcycle Safety Foundation. That's because the Rider-Course and Experienced RiderCourse that the MSF offers are the most important resources for any motorcyclist. To find a program in your area, check out the MSF at www.msf-usa.org/.

AEROSTICH

AEROSTICH MADE ITS NAME by pioneering synthetic riding suits, the kind that are worn by just about every serious Iron-Butt-type long-distance motorcyclist, but today the company offers everything from riding gear to electronic accessories to camping equipment. When you're talking serious long-distance motorcyclists, Aerostich owner Andy Goldfine is as hard-core as they come, and he personally makes certain that the products he offers to the motorcycling community are the best available. Check out Aerostich at www.aerostich.com/.

CORBIN SADDLES

MIKE CORBIN IS A personal friend of mine, but if I didn't know him from Adam, I'd still use his saddles. I think the fact that just about every serious long-distance rider uses a Corbin saddle whether they know Mike or not means that I'm not alone in this opinion. You can check out Corbin at www.corbin.com/.

THUNDERHEADER

PROBABLY NO MOTORCYCLE-RELATED TOPIC is more controversial right now than loud exhaust pipes. A lot of riders run straight pipes—that is, pipes with no sound baffling whatsoever—or nearly straight pipes that are too loud for use on public streets. At the same time most new motorcycles have such restrictive exhaust systems that their performance suffers, so most riders end up adding some sort of aftermarket exhaust system. I know I do, and for the last twenty-five years I've only used Thunderheaders. As far as I'm concerned these are the best exhaust systems on the market. You can check out their exhaust systems at www.thunderheader.net/.

ARLEN NESS

THROUGHOUT THIS BOOK I'VE advocated keeping your bike basically stock, but I was talking about functional changes, like altering the geometry of your motorcycle's frame or overbuilding the engine. I also like to keep my bikes looking businesslike, but that doesn't mean you can't sharpen up your bike's appearance with some decorative accessories. There's no better place to get quality customizing accessories than from my good friend Arlen Ness. He can sell you anything from a customized footpeg to a complete motorcycle. When you buy something from Arlen, you can be sure that it is the best-engineered, highest-quality part on the market. Check out the amazing range of products he offers at www.arlen-ness.com/.

TOTAL CONTROL ADVANCED RIDER CLINIC

EARLIER IN THE BOOK I suggested getting advanced rider training. Once you've finished the MSF Experienced RiderCourse, a good next step is Lee Parks's Total Control Advanced Rider Clinic. To see schedules and locations, go to www.totalcontroltraining.net/.

KLOCK WERKS KUSTOM CYCLES

WHEN A MAN BUILDS custom motorcycles and designs motorcycle parts in the middle of South Dakota, about 250 miles away from the edge of nowhere, he'd better be good at what he does, and Brian Klock, founder of Klock Werks Kustom Cycles, definitely meets that criteria. If you're in the market for anything from a well-designed part to a complete custom bike, Klock Werks has what you are looking for. Check them out at www.kustomcycles.com/.

READING LIST

IN WRITING THIS BOOK, I've tried my best to sum up the tricks and techniques I've learned over the course of a lifetime of riding, and I think I've done a good job of presenting information you're not going to find anywhere else, but there's still a lot of information that you won't find in these pages. It's a good thing other people have written about this subject, so that much of that information is available elsewhere. All of these books are available on Amazon.com. There are many bits of information in the following books that could very easily save your life, so you owe it to yourself to read them:

The Motorcycle Safety Foundation's Guide to Motorcycling Excellence: Skills, Knowledge, and Strategies for Riding Right (2nd ed.) by the Motorcycle Safety Foundation

This is the textbook for the MSF RiderCourse program, and as such, it should be as indispensable a part of your motorcycling experience as the RiderCourse itself.

How to Ride a Motorcycle: Rider's Guide to Strategy, Safety and Skill Development by Pat Hahn

Maximum Control: Mastering Your Heavyweight Bike by Pat Hahn

Ride Hard, Ride Smart: Ultimate Street Strategies for Advanced Motorcyclists by Pat Hahn

No book can really teach you how to ride a bike, but no book better prepares you to learn than Pat Hahn's *How to Ride a Motorcycle.* This is a good one to read before you take the MSF RiderCourse. *Maximum Control* focuses on the specific skills needed to master a heavyweight motorcycle, but it has a lot to offer the rider of any motorcycle, large or small. If the MSF RiderCourse is a freshman-level course, think of *Ride Hard, Ride Smart* as a sophomore-level textbook. It takes up where the RiderCourse leaves off, bridging the gap between the MSF material and high-performance riding books like *Total Control* and *Twist of the Wrist.*

Total Control by Lee Parks

Unlike most high-performance riding books, which focus on the needs of a race rider, this one applies the lessons to street riding.

A Twist of the Wrist: The Motorcycle Road Racers Handbook by Keith Code

Twist of the Wrist II: The Basics of High-Performance Motorcycle Riding by Keith Code

Soft Science of Road Racing Motorcycles: The Technical Procedures and Workbook for Road Racing Motorcycles by Keith Code

Keith Code's books were the first modern high-performance riding books, and in many ways they are still among the best. They are primarily focused on the demands of riding on a racetrack, but they still contain a lot of good information for anyone wanting to be a better rider.